teacher's friend publications

March!

a creative idea book
for the
elementary teacher

written and illustrated
by
Karen Sevaly

Copyright © Teacher's Friend,
a Scholastic Company
All rights reserved.
Printed in the U.S.A.

ISBN-13 978-0-439-50372-3
ISBN-10 0-439-50372-8

This book is dedicated
to teachers and children
everywhere.

Table of Contents

MAKING THE MOST OF IT! 7

    What Is in This Book 8
    How to Use This Book 8
    Adding the Color 9
    Lamination 9
    Photocopies and Ditto Masters 10
    Monthly Organizers 11
    Bulletin Board Ideas 11
    Lettering and Headings 12

CALENDAR - MARCH! 13

    March Calendar and Activities 14
    March Calendar Header 17
    March Calendar Symbols .18
    March - Blank Calendar 20

SPRING ACTIVITIES! 21

    Spring Activities! 22
    Spring Cleaning Promise! .23
    Spring Finger Puppets! 23
    Spring Cleaning! 24
    Spring Pencil Toppers 25
    Lion or Lamb 26
    Springtime Bingo! 28
    Bingo Words 29
    March Saying Puzzle 29
    March Bookmarks 30
    My Springtime Book! 31
    March Award 32
    Student of the Month 33
    Lamb Mask 34
    Lion Mask 35
    Spring Fever Visor 36

ST. PATRICK'S DAY! 37

    St. Patrick's Day 38
    Irish Fun! 39
    Shamrock Pattern 40
    My Leprechaun Book! 41
    International Children - Ireland 42
    Leprechaun Game Board .44
    Leprechaun Wheel 46
    Pot of Gold 48
    St. Patrick's Day Patterns .49
    Leprechaun Costume 50
    St. Patrick's Day Color Page 52

WEATHER! 53

    Weather Activities 54
    Rain or Shine Craft 56
    Weather Symbols 57
    Umbrella Paper Bag Puppet 58
    Today's Weather! 59
    Hanging Umbrella 60
    Reading Umbrella 61
    My Weather Wheel 62
    Weather Mobile 64
    Umbrella and Raindrop 66
    Weather Award! 67
    Windy Crafts! 67
    Pinwheel Pattern 68

WOMEN IN HISTORY! 69

    Famous Women Word Find! 70
    My Report on a Great Woman! 71
    Famous Women Concentration! 72
    Eleanor Roosevelt - Portrait 77
    Helen Keller - Portrait 78
    Sacagawea - Portrait 79
    Susan B. Anthony - Portrait 80
    Wilma Rudolph - Portrait 81
    Amelia Earhart - Portrait 92

MUSIC APPRECIATION! .83

    Music Month Activities! .84
    Musical Notes 86
    Singing Telegram 87
    Marching Band Hat 88
    Tuba Teddy 90
    Musical Word Find! 92
    Musical Instrument Match! 92

JAPAN! 95

    Japan - Japanese Poetry - Haiku 96
    Japanese Festivals! 97
    International Children - Japan 98
    Torii Gate 100
    Fish Kite 101
    Map of Japan 102
    Koi Fish Puppet 103
    Japanese Lantern 104
    Japanese Crafts! 105
    Pearl and Oyster 106

FARM ANIMALS! 107

    Farm Animals in the Classroom! 108
    Animal Families! 110
    Barnyard Bingo! 110
    Farm Animal Patterns 112
    Barn Pattern 113
    Piggy Booklet 114
    Matching Hen and Nest 115
    Pig Puppet 116
    Cow Puppet 117
    Duck Puppet 118
    Certificate of Achievement 119
    Cow Character 120

RAINBOW OF COLORS! 121

    Rainbow of Colors Activities! 122
    Color Palette 124
    My Personal Color Wheel 126
    Color Pages 127

BULLETIN BOARDS AND MORE! 133

    Bulletin Boards and More! 134
    Bulletin Board Murals! 138
    Kite Pattern 139
    Jam Jar Pattern 140
    Strawberry Pattern 141
    Frog Patterns 142
    Up, Up and Away! 143

ANSWER KEY! 144

Making the most of it!

WHAT IS IN THIS BOOK:

You will find the following in each monthly idea book from Teacher's Friend Publications:

1. A calendar listing every day of the month with a classroom idea and mention of special holidays and events.

2. At least four student awards to be sent home to parents.

3. Three or more bookmarks that can be used in your school library or given to students by you as "Super Student Awards."

4. Numerous bulletin board ideas and patterns pertaining to the particular month and seasonal activity.

5. Easy-to-make craft ideas related to the monthly holidays and special days.

6. Dozens of activities emphasizing not only the obvious holidays, but also the often-forgotten celebrations such as "Women in History" and "Music Appreciation Month."

7. Creative writing pages, crossword puzzles, word finds, booklet covers, games, paperbag puppets, literature lists and much more!

8. Scores of classroom management techniques and methods proven to motivate your students to improve behavior and classroom work.

HOW TO USE THIS BOOK:

Every page of this book may be duplicated for individual classroom use.

Some pages are meant to be copied or used as duplicating masters. Other pages may be transferred onto construction paper or used as they are.

If you have access to a print shop, you will find that many pages work well when printed on index paper. This type of paper takes crayons and felt markers well and is sturdy enough to last. (Bookmarks work particularly well on index paper.)

Lastly, some pages are meant to be enlarged with an overhead or opaque projector. When we say enlarge, we mean it! Think BIG! Three, four or even five feet is great! Try using colored butcher paper or posterboard so you don't spend all your time coloring.

ADDING THE COLOR:

Putting the color to finished items can be a real bother to teachers in a rush. Try these ideas:

1. On small areas, watercolor markers work great. If your area is rather large, switch to crayons or even colored chalk or pastels.

   (Don't worry, lamination or a spray fixative will keep color on the work and off you. No laminator or fixative? A little hair spray will do the trick.)

2. The quickest method of coloring large items is to start with colored paper. (Posterboard, butcher paper or large construction paper work well.) Add a few dashes of a contrasting colored marker or crayon and you will have it made.

3. Try cutting character eyes, teeth, etc. from white typing paper and gluing them in place. These features will really stand out and make your bulletin boards come alive.

   For special effects, add real buttons or lace. Metallic paper looks great on stars and belt buckles, too.

LAMINATION:

If you have access to a roll laminator, then you already know how fortunate you are. They are priceless when it comes to saving time and money. Try these ideas:

1. You can laminate more than just classroom posters and construction paper. Try various kinds of fabric, wallpaper and giftwrap. You'll be surprised at the great combinations you come up with.

   Laminated classified ads can be used to cut headings for current events bulletin boards. Colorful gingham fabric makes terrific cut letters or bulletin board trim. You might even try burlap! Bright foil giftwrap will add a festive feeling to any bulletin board.

   (You can even make professional looking bookmarks with laminated fabric or burlap. They are great holiday gift ideas for Mom or Dad!)

2. Felt markers and laminated paper or fabric can work as a team. Just make sure the markers you use are permanent and not water-based. Oops, made a mistake! That's okay. Put a little ditto fluid on a tissue, rub across the mark and presto, it's gone! Also, dry transfer markers work great on lamination and can easily be wiped off.

LAMINATION:
(continued)

3. Laminating cut-out characters can be tricky. If you have enlarged an illustration onto posterboard, simply laminate first and then cut it out with scissors or an art knife. (Just make sure the laminator is hot enough to create a good seal.)

One problem may arise when you paste an illustration onto posterboard and laminate the finished product. If your paste-up is not 100% complete, your illustration and posterboard may separate after laminating. To avoid this problem, paste your illustration onto posterboard that measures slightly larger than the illustration. This way, the lamination will help hold down your paste-up.

4. When pasting-up your illustration, always try to use either rubber cement, artist's spray adhesive or a glue stick. White glue, tape or paste does not laminate well because it can often be seen under your artwork.

5. Have you ever laminated student-made place mats, crayon shavings, tissue paper collages, or dried flowers? You'll be amazed at the variety of creative things that can be laminated and used in the classroom or as take-home gifts.

PHOTOCOPIES AND DITTO MASTERS:

Many of the pages in this book can be copied for use in the classroom. Try some of these ideas for best results:

1. If the print from the back side of your original comes through the front when making a photocopy or ditto master, slip a sheet of black construction paper behind the sheet. This will mask the unwanted shadows and create a much better copy.

2. Several potential masters in this book contain instructions for the teacher. Simply cover the type with correction fluid or a small slip of paper before duplicating.

3. When using a new ditto master, turn down the pressure on the duplicating machine. As the copies become light, increase the pressure. This will get longer wear out of both the master and the machine.

4. Trying to squeeze one more run out of that worn ditto master can be frustrating. Try lightly spraying the inked side of the master with hair spray. For some reason, this helps the master put out those few extra copies.

MONTHLY ORGANIZERS:

Staying organized month after month, year after year can be a real challenge. Try this simple idea:

After using the loose pages from this book, file them in their own file folder labeled with the month's name. This will also provide a place to save pages from other reproducible books along with craft ideas, recipes and articles you find in magazines. (*Essential Pocket Folders* by Teacher's Friend provide a perfect way to store your monthly ideas and reproducibles. Each *Monthly Essential Pocket Folder* comes with a sixteen-page booklet of essential patterns and organizational ideas. There are even special folders for *Back to School*, *The Substitute Teacher* and *Parent-Teacher Conferences*.)

You might also like to dedicate a file box for every month of the school year. A covered box will provide room to store large patterns, sample art projects, certificates and awards, monthly stickers, monthly idea books and much more.

BULLETIN BOARD IDEAS:

Creating clever bulletin boards for your classroom need not take fantastic amounts of time and money. With a little preparation and know-how, you can have different boards each month with very little effort. Try some of these ideas:

1. Background paper should be put up only once a year. Choose colors that can go with many themes and holidays. The black butcher-paper background you used as a spooky display in October will have a special dramatic effect in April with student-made, paper-cut butterflies.

2. Butcher paper is not the only thing that can be used to cover the back of your board. You might also try fabric from a colorful bed sheet or gingham material. Just fold it up at the end of the year to reuse again. Wallpaper is another great background cover. Discontinued rolls can be purchased for a small amount at discount hardware stores. Most can be wiped clean and will not fade like construction paper. (Do not glue wallpaper directly to the board; just staple or pin in place.)

3. Store your bulletin board pieces in large, flat envelopes made from two large sheets of tagboard or cardboard. Simply staple three sides together and slip the pieces inside. (Small pieces can be stored in ziploc bags.) Label your large envelopes with the name of the bulletin board and the month and year you displayed it. Take a picture of each bulletin board display. Staple the picture to your storage envelope. Next year when you want to create the same display, you will know where everything goes. Kids can even follow your directions when you give them a picture to look at.

LETTERING AND HEADINGS:

Not every school has a letter machine that produces perfect 4" letters. The rest of us will just have to use the old stencil-and-scissor method. But wait, there is an easier way!

1. Don't cut individual letters because they are difficult to pin up straight. Instead, hand print bulletin board titles and headings onto strips of colored paper. When it is time for the board to come down, simply roll it up to use again next year. If you buy your own pre-cut lettering, save yourself some time and hassle by pasting the desired statements onto long strips of colored paper. Laminate if possible. These can be rolled up and stored the same way!

   Use your imagination! Try cloud shapes and cartoon bubbles. They will all look great.

2. Hand-lettering is not that difficult, even if your printing is not up to penmanship standards. Print block letters with a felt marker. Draw big dots at the end of each letter. This will hide any mistakes and add a charming touch to the overall effect.

   If you are still afraid to freehand it, try this nifty idea: Cut a strip of posterboard about 28" X 6". Down the center of the strip, cut a window measuring 20" X 2" with an art knife . There you have it: a perfect stencil for any lettering job. All you need to do is write capital letters with a felt marker within the window slot. Don't worry about uniformity. Just fill up the entire window height with your letters. Move your posterboard strip along as you go. The letters will always remain straight and even because the posterboard window is straight.

3. If you must cut individual letters, use construction paper squares measuring 4 1/2" X 6". (Laminate first if you can.) Cut the capital letters as shown. No need to measure; irregular letters will look creative and not messy.

Calendar

March!

1ST The first NATIONAL PARK in the United States was established on this day in 1872. (Ask the students to find out which park was selected.)

2ND Today marks the birthdate of THEODORE GEISEL, whom we know as DR. SEUSS. (Ask your students to list as many of his books as they can.)

3RD Today is DOLLS' FESTIVAL DAY in Japan. (Ask all of your students to bring favorite dolls or stuffed toys from home to share with the class.)

4TH On this day in 1789, the UNITED STATES CONSTITUTION was put into effect. (Have students find out who was president at the time.)

5TH THE BOSTON MASSACRE, an attack by British troops on American colonists, took place on this day in 1770. Crispus Attucks, a black adventurer, was the first to be killed. (Students might like to find out more about Attucks.)

6TH "REMEMBER THE ALAMO!" This Texas fort in San Antonio, Texas, fell on this day in 1836 to General Santa Anna and his Mexican troops. (Ask students to find San Antonio on the classroom map.)

7TH American horticulturist LUTHER BURBANK was born on this day in 1849. (Ask students to find out what a horticulturist does and what Burbank discovered.)

8TH Today is INTERNATIONAL WOMEN'S DAY! (Ask each student to research a famous woman that they admire.)

9TH AMERIGO VESPUCCI, Italian navigator and explorer, was born on this day in 1454. (Encourage your students to find out what was named after this famous adventurer.)

10TH HARRIET TUBMAN, an escaped slave who helped free more than 300 other slaves, died on this day in 1913. (Ask your students to find out more about this great lady.)

11TH JOHN CHAPMAN, better known as JOHNNY APPLESEED, died on this day in 1847. (If you didn't celebrate his birthday in September, celebrate today by eating an apple with your class.)

12TH The GIRL SCOUTS was founded on this day in 1912. (Ask students to find out more about the organization's founder, Juliet Lowe.)

13TH The planet URANUS was discovered on this day in 1781 by the German-English astronomer SIR WILLIAM HERSCHEL. (Ask students to locate Uranus on a map of our solar system.)

14TH ALBERT EINSTEIN, Nobel Prize winner and father of atomic energy, was born on this day in 1879. (Have students find the meaning of the equation $E=mc^2$.)

15TH Today is known as the IDES OF MARCH, commemorating the assassination of Roman emperor Julius Caesar in 44 B.C. (Have students locate Rome, Italy on the classroom map.)

16TH JAMES MADISON, fourth president of the United States, was born on this day in 1751. (Instruct your students to find out about this president and his accomplishments in office.)

17TH Today is SAINT PATRICK'S DAY! (Wear green on this day to honor the Irish gentleman who is said to have driven the snakes out of Ireland.)

18TH The first person to walk in space was Soviet cosmonaut ALEXEI LEONOV on this day in 1965. (Ask students to find out which American was the first to walk in space.)

19TH Today marks the return of the SWALLOWS to Capsitrano, California. For more than 200 years, these birds have returned to the same location on this day, each year. (Have students find a picture of a swallow in a book at your school library.)

20TH SPRING officially begins today in the northern Hemisphere. (Have students find out which season begins in the southern Hemisphere.)

21ST Today marks the birthday of the German composer JOHANN SEBASTIAN BACH in 1685. (In celebration, play one of Bach's many symphonies.)

22ND The famous French mime MARCEL MARCEAU was born on this day in 1923. (Encourage your students to perform their own mime acts for the class.)

23RD "GIVE ME LIBERTY OR GIVE ME DEATH!" was said on this day in 1771, in a speech to the Continental Congress. (Have students find out who gave this famous speech.)

24TH Today is AGRICULTURE DAY in the United States. (Ask students to list all of the essential foods that come directly from the American farmer.)

25TH Today marks the birthdate of American sculptor BUTZON BORGLUM in 1871. He was the craftsman who created the presidential faces on Mt. Rushmore. (Ask students to find out which presidents are represented.)

26TH Happy birthday to Supreme Court justice SANDRA DAY O'CONNOR! She was born on this day in 1930. (Ask students what changes they would like to make if they were a Supreme Court justice.)

27TH A major EARTHQUAKE struck the state of Alaska on this day in 1963. (Practice "duck and cover" exercises with your students.)

28TH A nuclear power accident happened on this day in 1979 at THREE MILE ISLAND, Pennsylvania. (Ask students to list the advantages and disadvantages of nuclear power.)

29TH VIETNAM VETERAN'S DAY is celebrated on this day by many veterans of the Vietnam War. (Ask students to locate the country of Vietnam on the classroom map.)

30TH Dutch artist VINCENT VAN GOGH was born on this day in 1853. (Locate several prints of Van Gogh's paintings and display them on the class bulletin board.)

31ST The EIFFEL TOWER was officially opened on this day in 1889 during the World's Fair. (Ask students to find out which European city is home to the Eiffel Tower.)

MARCH IS ALSO.....

NATIONAL NUTRITION MONTH

YOUTH ART MONTH

AMERICAN RED CROSS MONTH

MUSIC IN OUR SCHOOLS MONTH

RETURN THOSE BORROWED BOOKS WEEK (first week of March)

NATIONAL WILDLIFE WEEK (third week of March)

TF0300 March Idea Book

March

Sunday	Monday	Tuesday	Wednesday	Thursday	Friday	Saturday

Spring Activities!

Spring Activities!

During the month of March, spring gently unfolds its colorful beauty. It's a wonderful time to appreciate nature and to admire the colors and freshness of the spring season. Try some of these activities with your students.

SPRING! SPRING! SPRING!
Ask your students to do one or more of these springtime activities:

• List six ways that spring is different from autumn.
• Ask six people what they like best about spring. Record the results and report your findings.
• Write a poem about spring using the letters S-P-R-I-N-G.
• Look up the word "spring" in the dictionary and list at least three different definitions.
• Write a story entitled, "The Year Spring Forgot to Come!"
• Find the times for both sunset and sunrise on March 21st (the first day of spring) in the local newspaper. Compare these times to those from one or two weeks ago.

SPRING CLEANING!
Encourage students to keep their desk and work area neat and tidy by arranging a "spring cleaning" afternoon. Tell the children when the spring cleaning will take place. Provide a bottle of spray cleaner and paper towels to clean the desk tops and paper grocery bags so students can take personal things home. Have students take an inventory of the things found in their desks. (Use the form provided in this chapter.) The results of the inventory can be used in graphing exercises.

BLOWING BUBBLES!
Reward your students for jobs well done by letting them blow bubbles!

Give each student a small, empty baby food jar with lid. Fill each jar two-thirds full with water and add two teaspoons of liquid detergent. Provide several different colors of food coloring and let each child pick their favorite to color their mixture. This activity shows how mixing primary colors will make secondary colors. (Red and yellow make orange, yellow and blue make green, and blue and red make purple.)

Stir the solution until mixed. Instruct each student to make a bubble wand by bending a pipe cleaner to form a loop and handle. Students dip the wands into the jar and blow the bubbles. See who can make the biggest bubbles.

Spring Cleaning Promise!

I promise to:
- Keep my desk and work area clean and tidy.
- Make sure that the supplies I need are in good shape and ready to use.
- Do my work as neatly as possible and turn it in on time.

_____
Date

_____
Student's Signature

Spring Finger Puppets!

Cut Out

Cut Out

Cut Out

Cut Out

TF0300 March Idea Book

Spring Cleaning!

_____
Student's Name

"My Clean Desk Inventory!"

While cleaning my desk, I found the following items:

Quantity	Items	Quantity	Items
_____	pencils	_____	textbooks (list titles)
_____	crayons	_____
_____	erasers	_____
_____	blank paper	
_____	notebooks	_____ reading/library books
_____	folders	(list titles)
_____	completed work papers	_____
_____	incomplete work papers	_____
_____	_____	_____
_____	_____	

I found these following personal items: _____

_____

_____

_____

_____

_____

It's important that I am prepared to do my work and learn at school. To achieve this I will do the following: _____

_____

_____

_____

_____

Spring Pencil Toppers

Reproduce these "Pencil Toppers" onto construction or index paper. Color and cut out. Use an art knife to cut through the Xs.

Slide a pencil through both Xs, as shown.

Give them as classroom awards or birthday treats.

     TF0300 March Idea Book

Lion or Lamb

Cut these two patterns from colored paper. Color and paste each lion and lamb pattern to the centers of two paper plates. Now, staple the plates together, back to back.

Glue a tongue depressor between the plates, as shown, for a handle. Or, attach a string to the top of the plates and hang as a two-sided mobile.

26

Glue cotton batting or cotton balls to the lamb pattern. Paste stick pretzels, short sections of yarn or dry spaghetti to form the lion's mane.

SPRINGTIME
BINGO

FREE

Springtime Bingo!

Your students will enjoy learning more about spring with this springtime bingo game. Give each child a copy of the bingo words listed below or write the words on the chalkboard. Ask students to write any 24 words on his or her bingo card. Use the same directions you might use for regular bingo.

SPRINGTIME BINGO WORDS

MARCH	PLANTS	BEES	ANIMALS
BEAUTY	DAISIES	BUTTERFLIES	BABIES
FLOWERS	ROSES	BUGS	BIRTH
BLOSSOM	POPPIES	WEATHER	LAMB
BLOOM	PANSIES	RAIN	CALF
BUDS	SPROUT	SUNSHINE	COLT
LEAVES	COLOR	UMBRELLA	CHICK
SEEDS	NEW	CLOUDS	BIRDS
FIELDS	FRESH	SHOWERS	HATCH
WILDFLOWERS	INSECTS	DEW	EGGS

This bingo game can also be used to teach vocabulary words or math facts.

March Saying!

An old saying about the month of March is hidden in the even-numbered blocks.

ACTIVITY 1

1. B	2. M	3. T	4. A	5. L	6. R	7. F	8. C	9. M	10. H	11. N	12. C	13. B	14. O	15. C
16. M	17. O	18. E	19. N	20. S	21. P	22. I	23. R	24. N	25. S	26. L	27. F	28. I	29. G	30. K
31. X	32. E	33. P	34. A	35. P	36. L	37. G	38. I	39. N	40. O	41. M	42. N	43. H	44. A	45. E
46. N	47. F	48. D	49. B	50. G	51. E	52. O	53. R	54. E	55. T	56. S	57. Q	58. O	59. P	60. U
61. M	62. T	63. B	64. L	65. F	66. I	67. S	68. K	69. T	70. E	71. R	72. A	73. P	74. L	75. L
76. A	77. G	78. M	79. H	80. B										

Can you figure out what it says? Write it below.

_____

_____

_____

Read about...

Leprechauns

... in the Library!

RISE AND SHINE BY READING A BOOK!

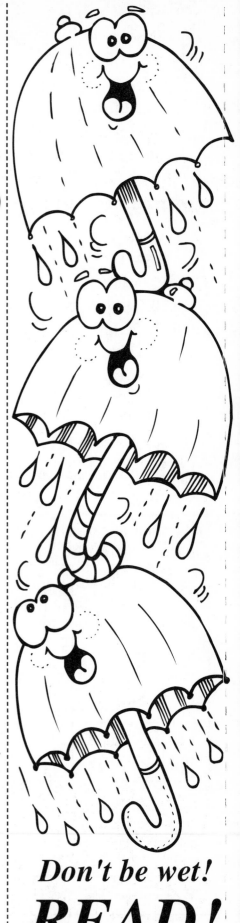

Don't be wet!
READ!

TF0300 March Idea Book

Name

FOLD

My
Springtime
Book!

TF0300 March Idea Book

Name

was a ray
of sunshine
today!

Date

Teacher

No "lion," you did a great job!

Date

Teacher

Name

was uplifting
in class today!

Teacher   Date

Name

was a
real <u>lamb</u> in class today!

Date

Teacher

STUDENT
OF THE
MONTH

NAME

SCHOOL

DATE

TEACHER

Cut Out

Cut Out

Lamb Mask

TF0300 March Idea Book

Cut
Out

Cut
Out

Lion
Mask

TF0300 March Idea Book

Spring Fever Visor

Copy this visor onto sturdy index or construction paper. Children can do the coloring.

Punch holes at both ends and attach string elastic. (With elastic, the students can easily remove the visor without retying.)

If you wish to save on the cost of elastic, simply use mailing string. Either way, the kids will love them and so will you!

SPRING!

Name

St. Patrick's Day!

St. Patrick's Day is celebrated each March 17th in honor of Ireland's patron saint, Saint Patrick.

Patrick was born to wealthy parents in England, about 385 A.D. His full name was Magonus Sucatus Patricius. Legend has it that when Patrick was sixteen years old, he was kidnapped by Irish pirates and eventually sold as a slave.

For several years, Patrick may have worked as a shepherd in northern Ireland. It was during this time that he decided to devote his life to Christ and teach the Irish his faith. After much hardship, it is said that Patrick escaped his captors and fled to France where he began studying for the priesthood. He soon returned to Ireland, where he taught the Irish to read and write along with the teachings of Christianity.

It is believed that Saint Patrick was responsible for bringing the small shamrock plant to Ireland. He often used the shamrock in his sermons to illustrate the message of the holy trinity. Today the shamrock is the national flower of Ireland.

Most historians do not believe the many stories about St. Patrick. But one thing is sure, on March 17th, with many festive gatherings and much merrymaking around the world, everyone is Irish!

LEPRECHAUNS

As legend states, every leprechaun has a pot of gold hidden in a secret place. If captured, he must give up his golden treasure. Of course, it's quite difficult to catch a leprechaun. They are especially tricky and can often turn themselves into rabbits or squirrels to fool you into thinking they are something they aren't. When they are caught, however, they often trick their captor into looking away for a split second, so that they can escape into the woods.

One tale is told of an Irish gentleman who, after much searching and effort, captured one of the wee folk. After much coaxing, the Irishman finally persuaded the leprechaun to take him to the very bush where his treasure of gold was buried. It is said that the man quickly tied a red bandanna to a branch on the bush and hurried home to fetch a shovel. When he returned a short time later to dig up his treasure, red bandanna had been fastened to every bush in the forest.

Leprechauns love to play tricks on people, causing them to drop or spill things. They often hide keys and other belongings, just to frustrate us. So next time you lose a possession that you swear should be right where you left it, don't be surprised if it's only some silly leprechaun having fun and playing tricks to pass the time.

Irish Fun!

Cut out

Cut out

IRISH JIG

Play a recording of a lively Irish tune and teach your class a traditional Irish jig. Follow these simple instructions:

Place hands on hips, feet together.

Hop on your right foot while placing your left foot in front, heel down.

Hop again and point your left toe in front of your right foot.

Hop a third time and return the left foot to the front, heel down.

Fourth hop returns you to the starting position.

Repeat the steps, hopping on your left foot.

LEPRECHAUN FINGER PUPPET

MATCH THESE IRISH WORDS TO THEIR MEANINGS!   ACTIVITY 2

GAELIC   Lively Irish dance

BLARNEY STONE   Ireland

IRISH JIG   Irish language

SHENANIGAN   Walking stick

GNOME   Mischief or trickery

SHILLELAGH   Kiss it and receive good luck

ERIN   Dwarf that guards a precious treasure

Shamrock Pattern

FOLD

My Leprechaun Book!

_____
Name

Ireland

42

Ireland

TEACHERS: Up to four children can play this game. Make your own task cards or write math problems to be solved on each shamrock.

Help the leprechaun find the pot of gold!

Cut
Out

Cut
Out

Copy this "Leprechaun
Wheel" onto heavy index paper.
Color, cut out and assemble with brass fasteners.
Cut out the two boxes, as shown.

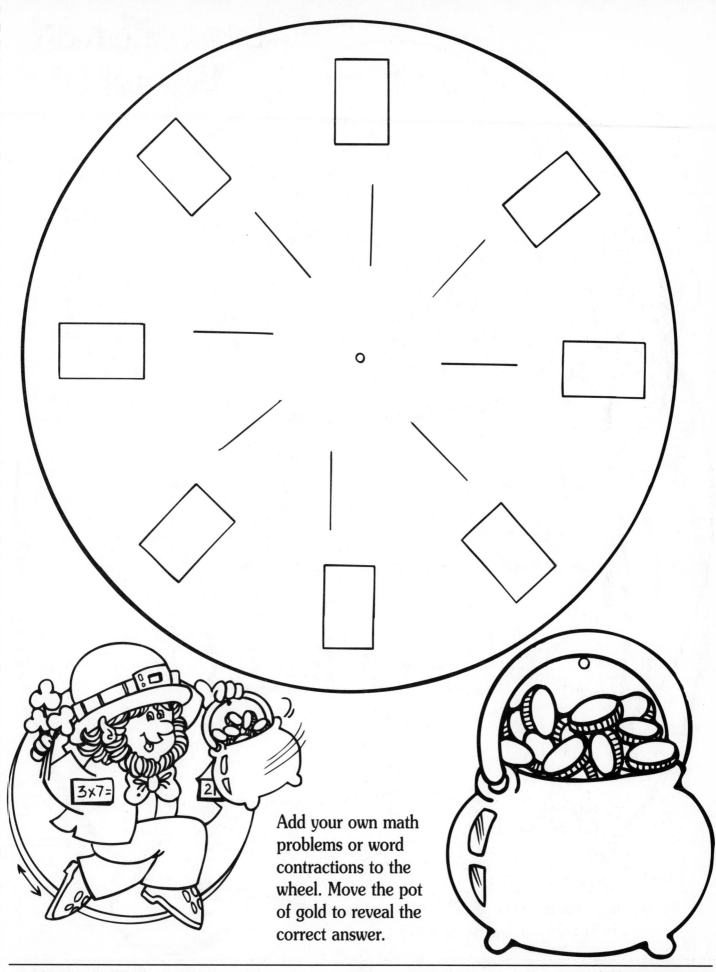

Add your own math problems or word contractions to the wheel. Move the pot of gold to reveal the correct answer.

47

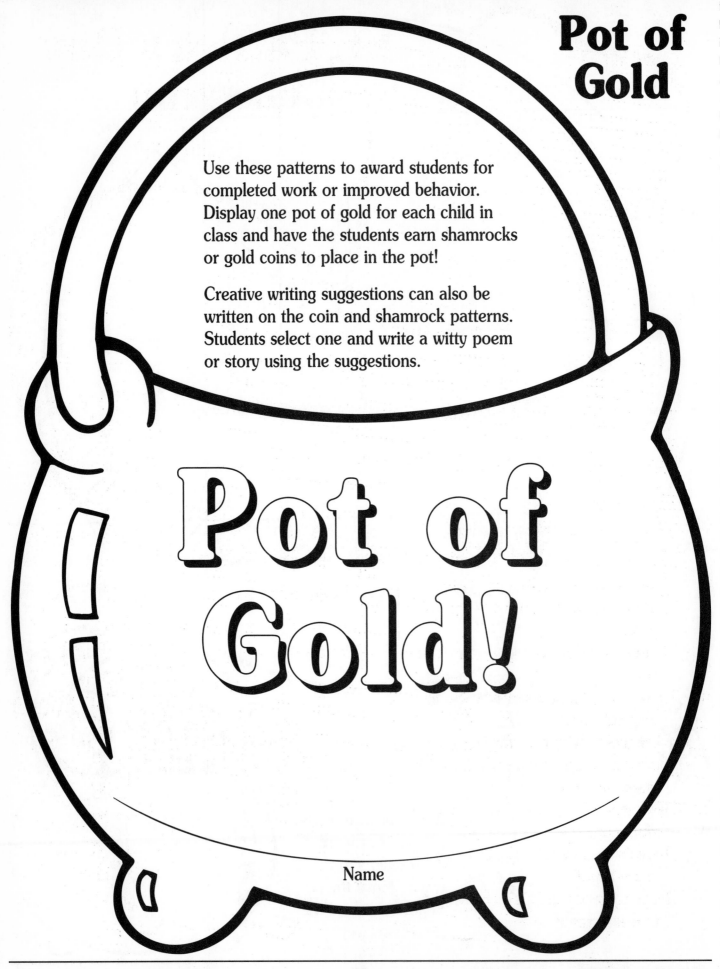

Use these patterns to award students for completed work or improved behavior. Display one pot of gold for each child in class and have the students earn shamrocks or gold coins to place in the pot!

Creative writing suggestions can also be written on the coin and shamrock patterns. Students select one and write a witty poem or story using the suggestions.

Pot of Gold!

Name

St. Patrick's Day Patterns

Creative Writing Ideas

- There was a leprechaun who forgot where he hid the pot of gold!
- There was a king who loved the color green!
- There was a troll who stole the blarney stone!
- There was a leprechaun who made a magical soup!
- There was a fairy who forgot how to fly!
- There was a leprechaun who lost his magic powers!
- There was a leprechaun who couldn't stop laughing!
- There was a boy who wanted to be a leprechaun!
- There was a leprechaun who forgot to wear green!

Leprechaun Costume

Children will love dressing up as a leprechaun on March 17th.

Cut this beard pattern from brown construction paper. Curl the ends around the child's ears to hold in place. Cut the ears from pink or green construction paper and paste or staple to the beard pattern to cover the child's ears.

You can also make a green paper leprechaun hat and a paper mustache to wear on St. Patrick's Day.

(Girls in the class may want to make only the hat and ears to wear as a leprechaun costume.)

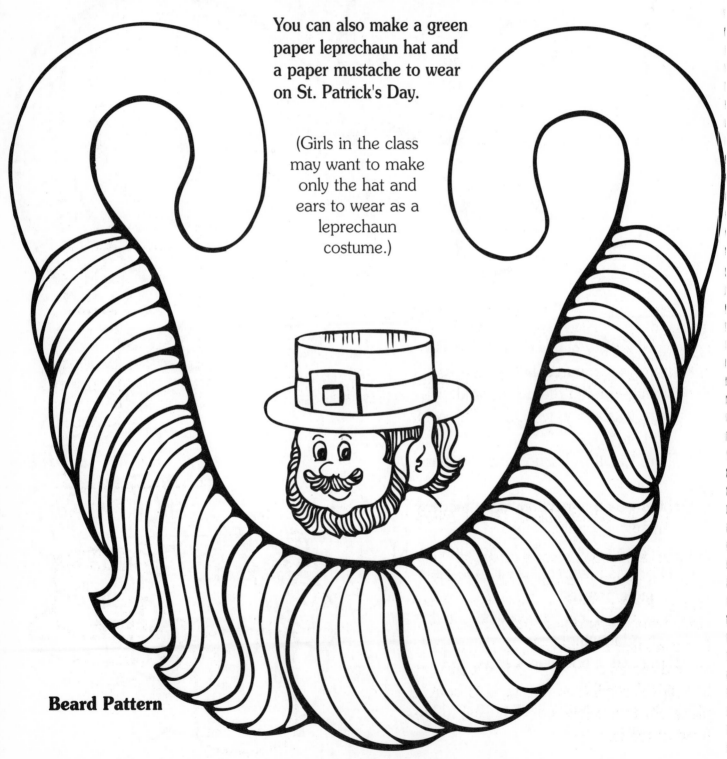

Beard Pattern

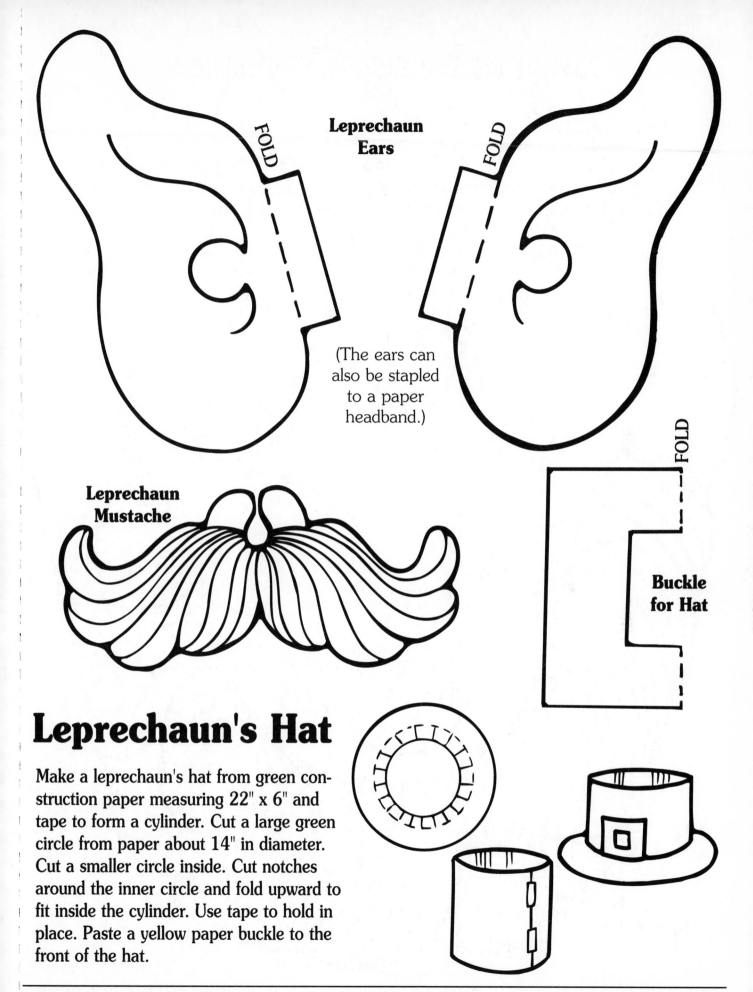

Leprechaun Ears

FOLD

FOLD

(The ears can also be stapled to a paper headband.)

Leprechaun Mustache

FOLD

Buckle for Hat

Leprechaun's Hat

Make a leprechaun's hat from green construction paper measuring 22" x 6" and tape to form a cylinder. Cut a large green circle from paper about 14" in diameter. Cut a smaller circle inside. Cut notches around the inner circle and fold upward to fit inside the cylinder. Use tape to hold in place. Paste a yellow paper buckle to the front of the hat.

St. Patrick's
Day
Coloring Page

Weather!

Weather Activities!

WEATHER EXPERIMENTS

Help your children understand various weather changes and some of the ways in which the weather is forecasted with these simple experiments.

THERMOMETER READINGS

Place a thermometer in a bowl of ice water. Let the children read the temperature. Place the same thermometer in warm water and have the students record the temperature each day for two weeks. Record the results, in graph form, on a chart.

EVAPORATION

Measure out identical amounts of water into two separate shallow containers. Put one container in a cool place and the other one in a warm, sunny location. After several hours, pour the water back into the measuring cups. Ask the children to observe if one container has more water than the other. Explain how water evaporates, condenses into clouds and eventually returns to earth in the form of rain, snow, etc.

MAKE A CLOUD

Freeze ice cubes in a metal tray. Fill a wide-mouthed jar with an inch of very hot water and set the tray of ice cubes on top of the jar. Darken the room and ask the students to observe the jar with a flashlight. They will soon see how the steam from the hot water hits the ice cube tray and forms a cloud inside the jar. Explain that this same thing happens when the warm moisture rises from earth and meets the cold air in the sky. The results are clouds!

WINDY DISCUSSIONS

Write these "windy" sayings on the class board and ask students to discuss their meanings. Encourage them to be creative in their explanations before you reveal their true meanings.

When something is "written on the wind" it is not very lasting.

When something is "blowing in the wind," there is something that will soon be known by everyone.

"To throw caution to the winds" means that someone is being reckless.

"Going before the wind" means that everything is proceeding smoothly.

A "windbag" is someone who talks all the time and says very little.

To "get wind" of something is to hear about something going on.

KITE CONTESTS

Arrange a kite-flying tournament for the children in your classroom.

Post a set of rules noting the types of kites that can be flown, time involved getting each kite into the air, etc. Provide ribbons and awards for the winners of the selected categories.

You might want to ask students to make their own kites. Ribbons can be awarded for most original kite, easiest kite to fly, highest-flying kite, etc.

Weather Activities!

THUNDER AND LIGHTNING

Children are always fascinated by the flash of lightning and the roar of thunder. They often want to know the storm's proximity. Here is a way they can compute this.

Begin by explaining the difference between the speed of light and the speed of sound. Ask them to count the seconds between the lightning and the sound of thunder and then use the following scale to estimate the distance.

Time Between Lightning/ Thunder	Distance of Lightning Flash
0 seconds	0 miles
5	1
10	2
15	3
20	4
25	5
30	6

...and so on.

RAINY DAY VOCABULARY

Ask students to draw or paint pictures of rainy day scenes and cover the class bulletin board with their creations. Next, cut out large, blue paper raindrops and label each one with a "rainy" vocabulary word, such as drizzle, mist, shower, sprinkle, cloudburst, thunderstorm, moisture, monsoon, hurricane, etc. Give one raindrop to each student and ask them to research the word and write its definition on the raindrop. Pin the complete raindrops to the bulletin board for a visual shower of vocabulary words.

WEATHER DISASTERS

Discuss with your class the various types of weather disasters such as tornadoes, floods, hurricanes, severe cold, drought, etc. Try some of these activities to help them understand severe weather conditions:

• Using the previous year's almanac, find the dates and locations of major weather disasters. Mark the areas on the class map.

• Write to your local weather bureau and ask them for information concerning the types of severe weather that are possible in your area.

• Ask a local radio or television weather reporter to visit your class. Have them explain how they gather and report weather news.

• Write to a relief agency (such as the Red Cross) to learn how to prepare for weather emergencies.

• Find out about the role of the National Guard when a natural disaster occurs.

RAINY DAY SENSES

Discuss with your class the various things they see, hear, smell or feel on a rainy day. These can include wet grass, thunder, lightning, etc. Ask students to write poems about the many things discussed.

Rain or Shine Craft

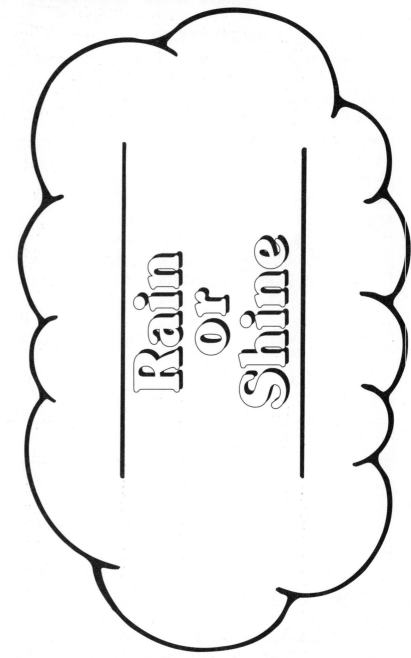

Cut these two patterns from heavy paper and color.
Cut the two slits with an art knife. Move up or down
to show the day's weather.

Weather Symbols

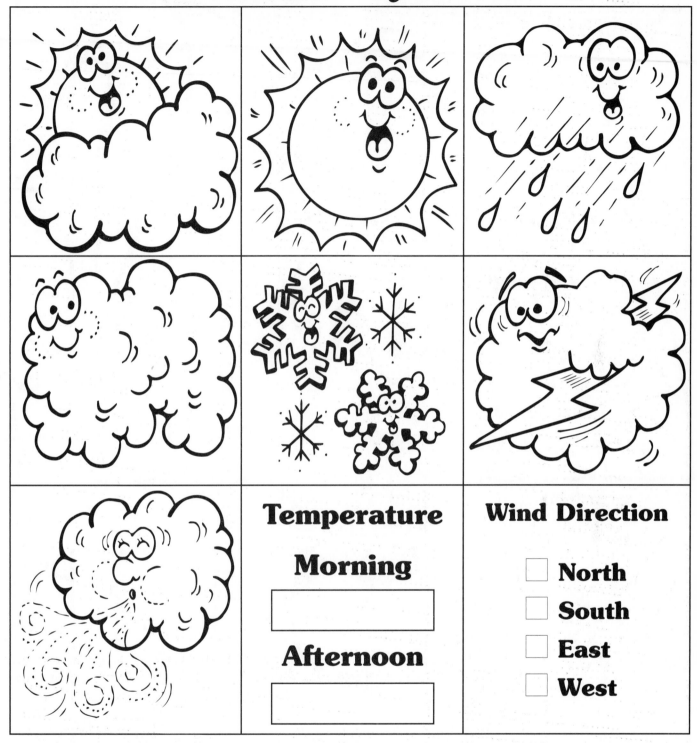

Temperature

Morning

Afternoon

Wind Direction

☐ **North**

☐ **South**

☐ **East**

☐ **West**

Use these weather cards to create an informative bulletin board in your classroom. Each morning, ask a child to go outside and describe the weather to the class. Have the child choose the appropriate weather symbol and attach it to the class calendar. The student should also record the temperature and the wind direction. Later in the afternoon, ask another child to follow the same procedure. Discuss these weather changes with your class. Older children might like to bring in the weather section of the local newspaper and compare their predictions and the accuracy of the weather reporters with the actual conditions.

Umbrella Paperbag Puppet

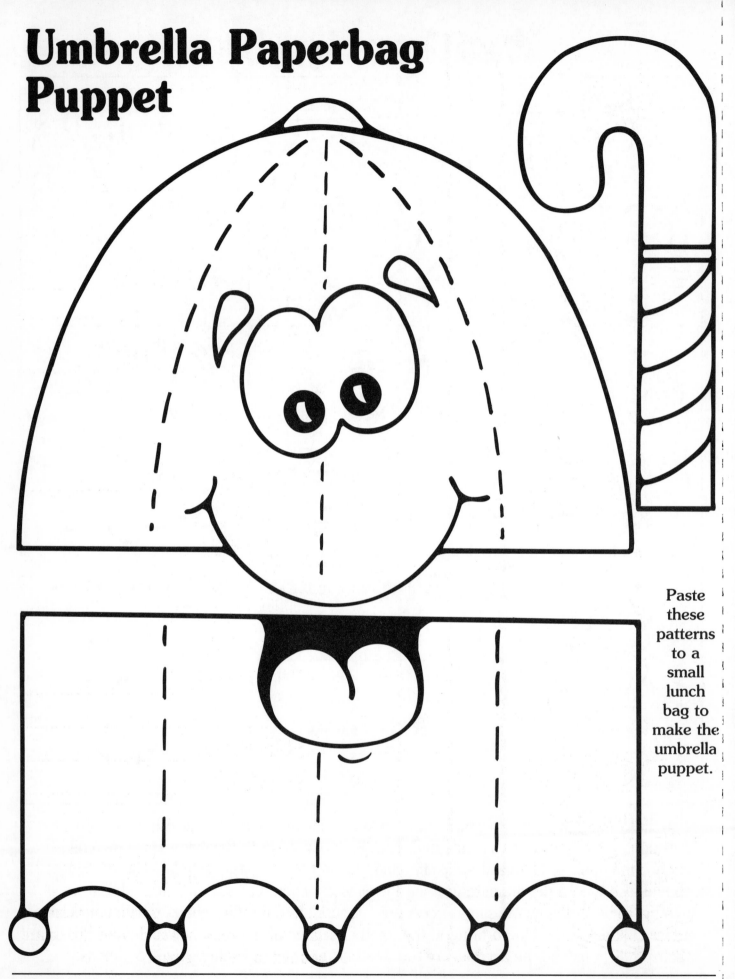

Paste these patterns to a small lunch bag to make the umbrella puppet.

TF0300 March Idea Book

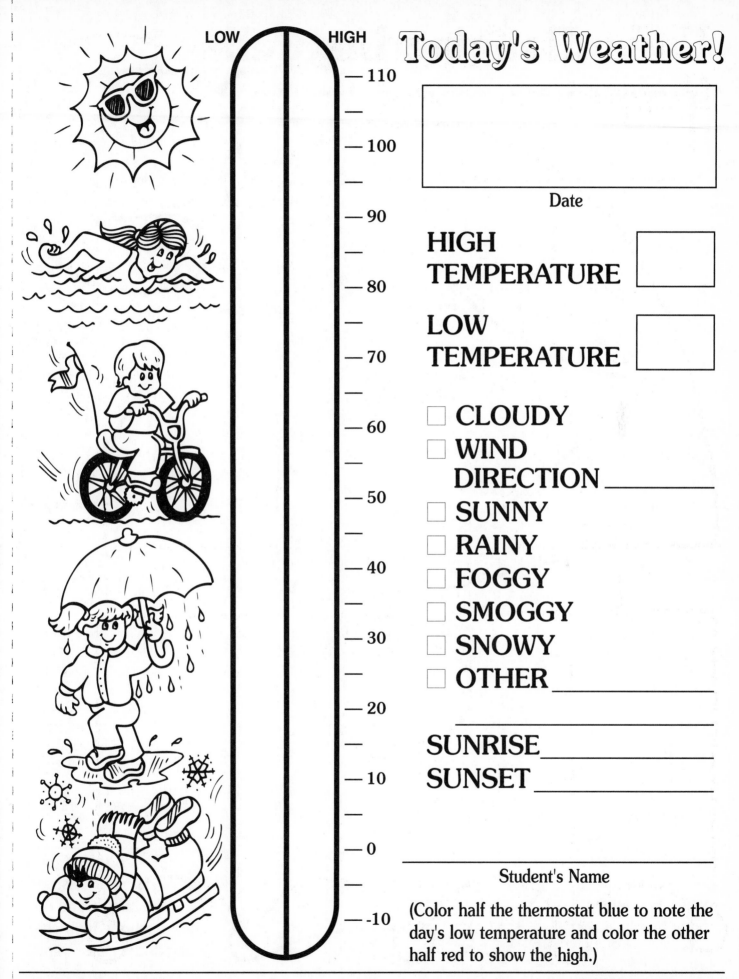

LOW HIGH

— 110
—
— 100
—
— 90
—
— 80
—
—
— 70
—
— 60
—
— 50
—
— 40
—
— 30
—
— 20
—
— 10
—
— 0
—
— -10

Today's Weather!

Date

HIGH
TEMPERATURE

LOW
TEMPERATURE

☐ CLOUDY
☐ WIND
 DIRECTION _____
☐ SUNNY
☐ RAINY
☐ FOGGY
☐ SMOGGY
☐ SNOWY
☐ OTHER_____
_____
SUNRISE_____
SUNSET _____

_____
Student's Name

(Color half the thermostat blue to note the day's low temperature and color the other half red to show the high.)

Hanging Umbrella

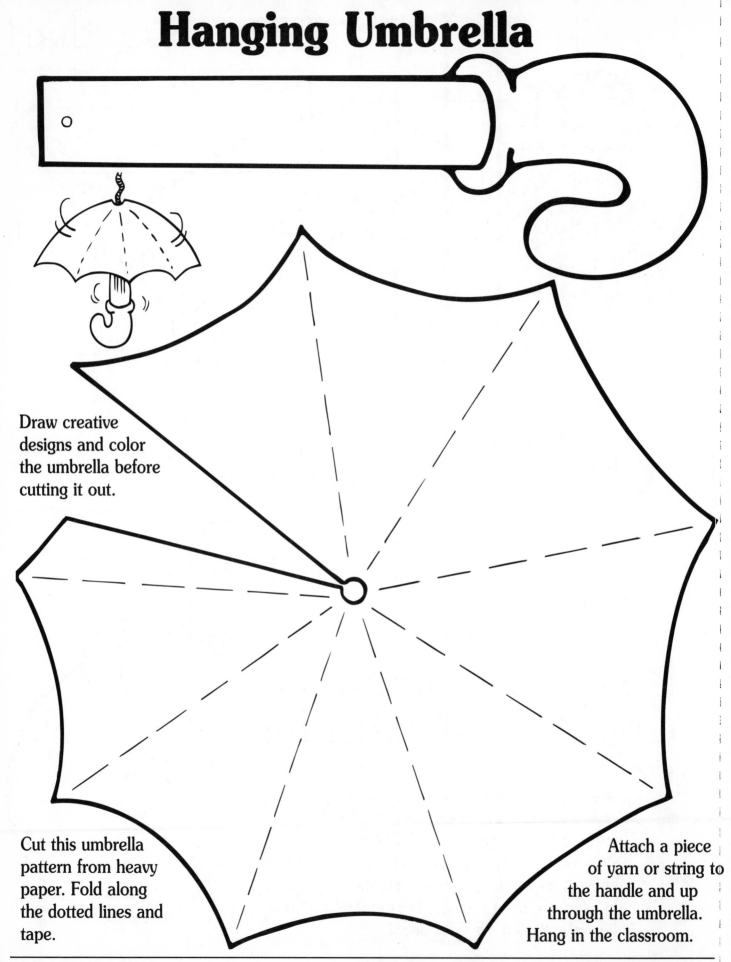

Draw creative designs and color the umbrella before cutting it out.

Cut this umbrella pattern from heavy paper. Fold along the dotted lines and tape.

Attach a piece of yarn or string to the handle and up through the umbrella. Hang in the classroom.

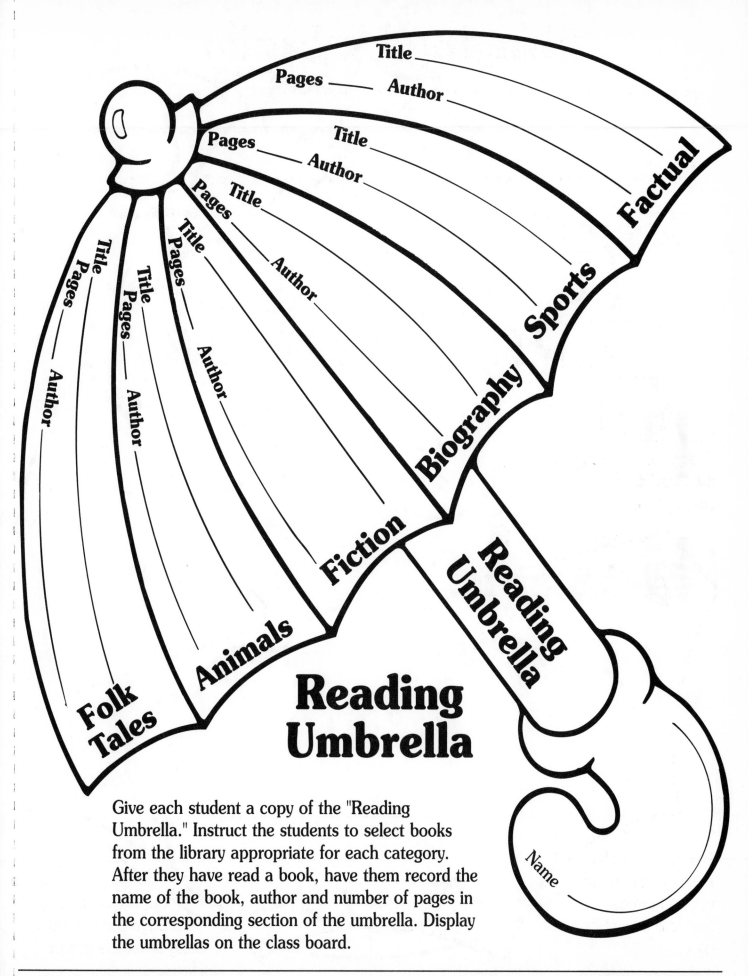

Reading Umbrella

Title
Author
Pages

Factual

Sports

Biography

Fiction

Animals

Folk Tales

Reading Umbrella

Name

Give each student a copy of the "Reading Umbrella." Instruct the students to select books from the library appropriate for each category. After they have read a book, have them record the name of the book, author and number of pages in the corresponding section of the umbrella. Display the umbrellas on the class board.

My Weather Wheel

Today's Weather is:

Cut out

Name

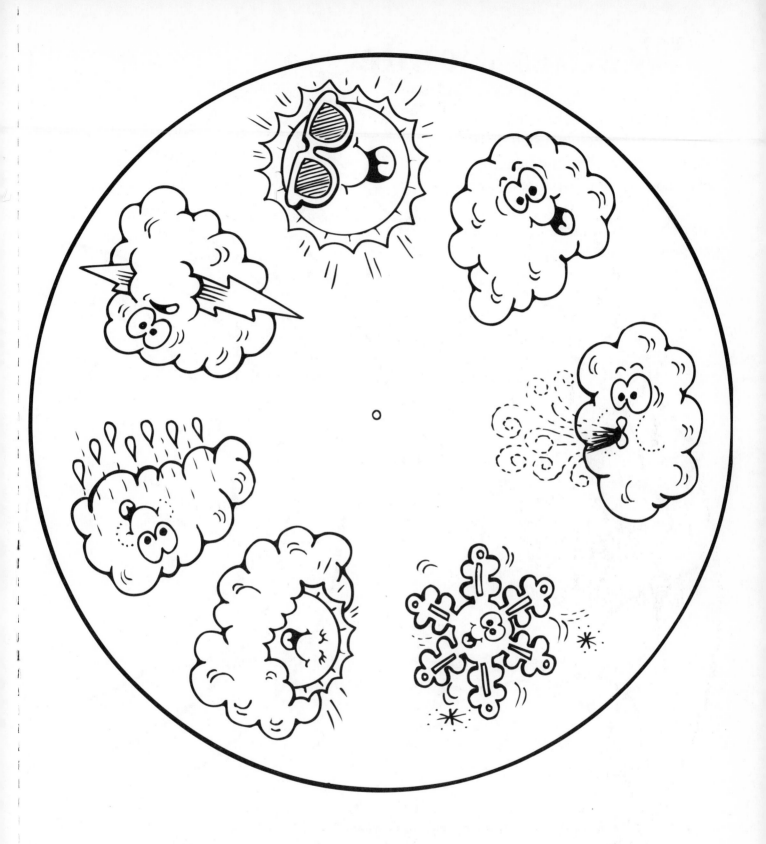

Cut these weather-wheel patterns from heavy paper. Color with crayons or markers. Cut out the area indicated. Assemble with a brass fastener and move the wheel to show the weather each day.

Weather Mobile

Each student can make his or her own "Weather Mobile" using these simple patterns. Cut the patterns from construction paper and assemble with thread or yarn, as shown. (For best results, paste the rainbow pattern to posterboard.)

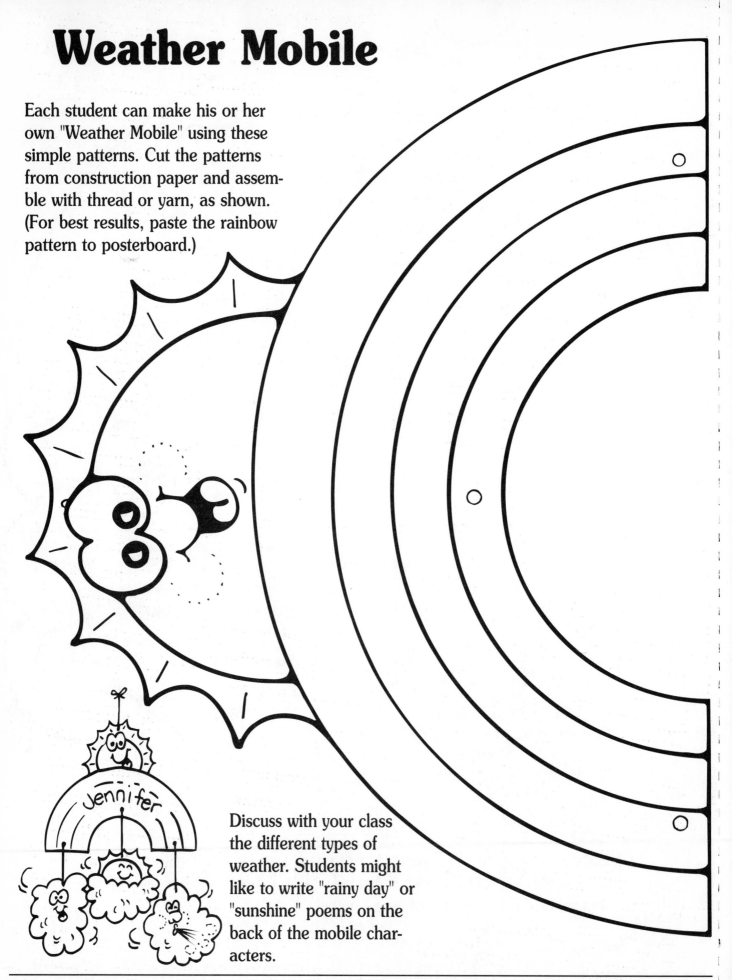

Discuss with your class the different types of weather. Students might like to write "rainy day" or "sunshine" poems on the back of the mobile characters.

TF0300 March Idea Book

Christmas tinsel taped to the back of a cloud is a clever way to represent rain, and silver foil glued to the lightning creates a dramatic effect. Students will love to experiment with a wide variety of materials.

Children will love to take this "Weather Mobile" home to share with family members.

Umbrella and Raindrop

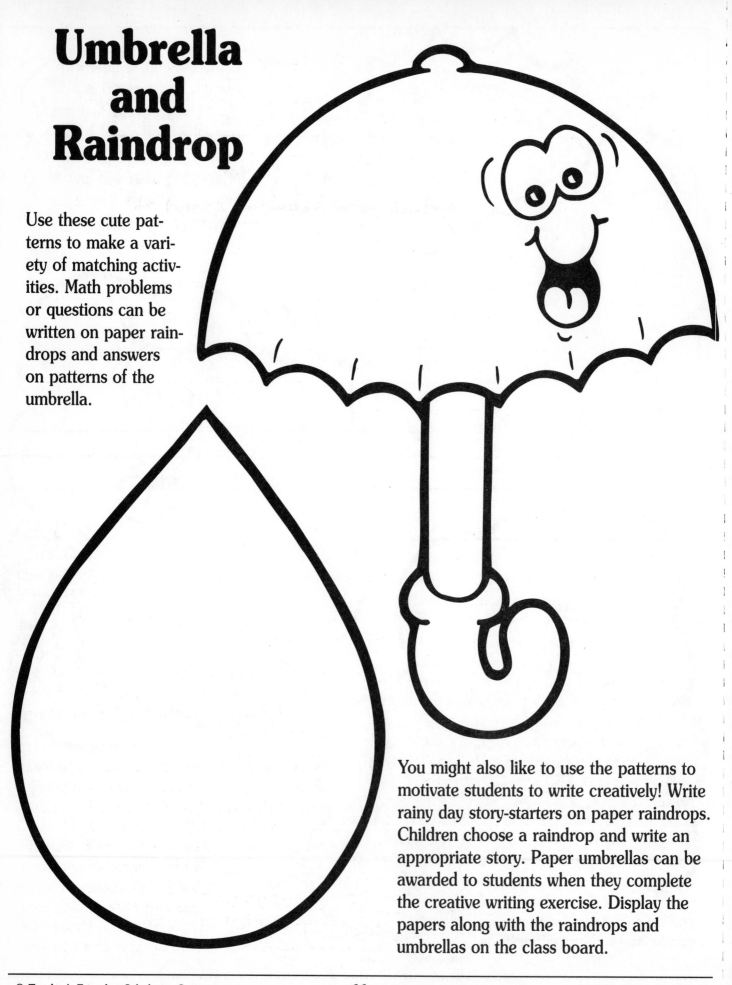

Use these cute patterns to make a variety of matching activities. Math problems or questions can be written on paper raindrops and answers on patterns of the umbrella.

You might also like to use the patterns to motivate students to write creatively! Write rainy day story-starters on paper raindrops. Children choose a raindrop and write an appropriate story. Paper umbrellas can be awarded to students when they complete the creative writing exercise. Display the papers along with the raindrops and umbrellas on the class board.

Weather Award!

_____
Name

_____

_____

_____   _____
Date   Teacher

- -

Windy Crafts!

WIND SOCKS

Give each child in class a small paper bag. Ask students to cut the bottom from the bag and decorate it with various weather symbols. Instruct the students to cut six 12" strips of colorful tissue paper and paste them to the edge of the bottom of the bag. Punch four holes, 1/2" from the edge, through the top of the bag. Space the holes equally around the edge. Cut four 12" pieces of yarn and one 24" piece. Tie the four pieces of yarn to the four holes. Gather the ends together and tie with the 24" piece. Tie the wind socks outside to a pole and have your children observe how they twist and turn as the direction of the wind changes. Small children can hold the wind socks and run to make them fill with air.

WIND CHIMES

This fun craft also makes an excellent Mother's or Father's Day gift!

For every child in class, collect one aluminum pie tin, three 8" pieces of string and 30 plastic or wooden beads.

Begin by having the children knot the ends of the strings. Have them string ten beads onto each string. Punch three holes in the center of the pie tin, pull the strings through the holes and tie the ends. Punch three more holes at the edge of the bottom of the tin and attach three long pieces of string. Hang outdoors in view of a window.

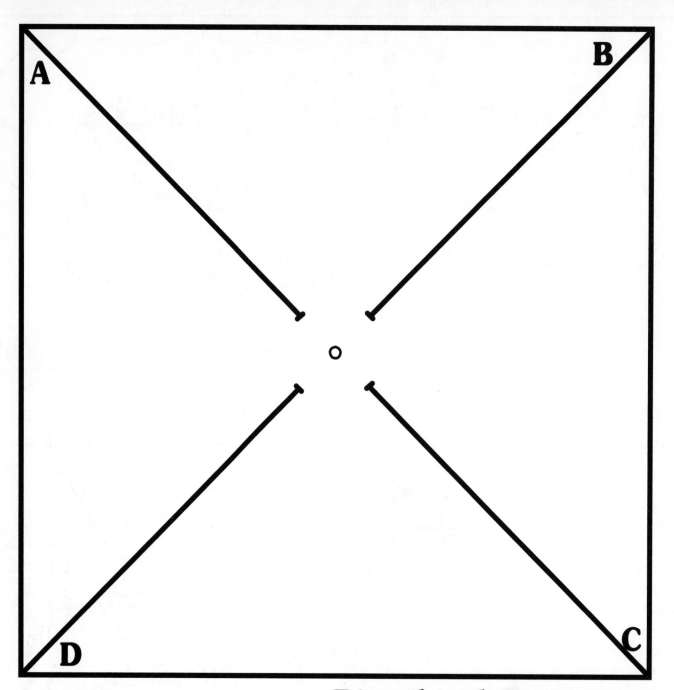

A   B

o

D   C

Pinwheel Pattern

Cut this pinwheel pattern from construction paper and decorate both sides using crayons or colored markers.

Cut along each corner line toward the center, stopping where indicated. Bend each corner (A,B,C, and D) to the center and secure with a straight pin. (Do not fold flat.)

Push the pin into an eraser at the end of a pencil and your pinwheel is ready to spin in the wind!

Women in History!

Famous Women Word Find!

ACTIVITY 3

FIND THE LAST NAMES OF THESE FAMOUS WOMEN IN THE PUZZLE BELOW:

Mary McLeod BETHUNE	Betsy ROSS	Harriet TUBMAN
Abigail ADAMS	Clara BARTON	Rosa PARKS
Coretta KING	Amelia EARHART	Katherine HEPBURN
Susan B. ANTHONY	Elizabeth BLACKWELL	Shirley Temple BLACK
Laura Ingalls WILDER	SACAGAWEA	Ramona BANUELOS
Sandra Day O'CONNOR	"Babe" DIDRIKSON	Wilma RUDOLPH
Sally RIDE	Helen KELLER	Pearl BUCK
Shirley CHISHOLM	Eleanor ROOSEVELT	Sojourner TRUTH

```
C V G T Y H J N T D C V B L A C K W E L L
H I D R D F G T Y H J U I K L O P M N H Y
I X C U D V K E L L E R S X A W V D R T H
S D E T I S F B U C K F T H Y U K I L O P
H S W H D S V B T S I S W E T U B M A N U
O S W E R D F G T Y N H E P B U R N D W Q
L W S R I S W V B N G H Y F R T Y H N M R
M C B N K D R F V R O O S E V E L T S C I
B A R X S B A R T O N C C V T Y H U J D D
S D O D O X V F G B A N U E L O S S W G E
C T S F N H W I L D E R S P A E W R T H Y
X Z S D F G B E T H U N E A B L A C K P R
R U D O L P H C F G S E T R V B N M K A I
A E A R H A R T S C F T Y K C V B N M R L
Z C D B G H S A C A G A W E A D C V B K Y
S D A V G T Y H J U I K L O P M B G Y S R
B V M A N T H O N Y V T Y U I R E W F D S
M K S F G B H N M J K L I U O C O N N O R
```

SELECT ONE OF THE WOMEN LISTED ABOVE AND WRITE A BRIEF DESCRIPTION OF HER ACCOMPLISHMENTS.

_____

_____

_____

_____

_____

My Report On A Great Woman!

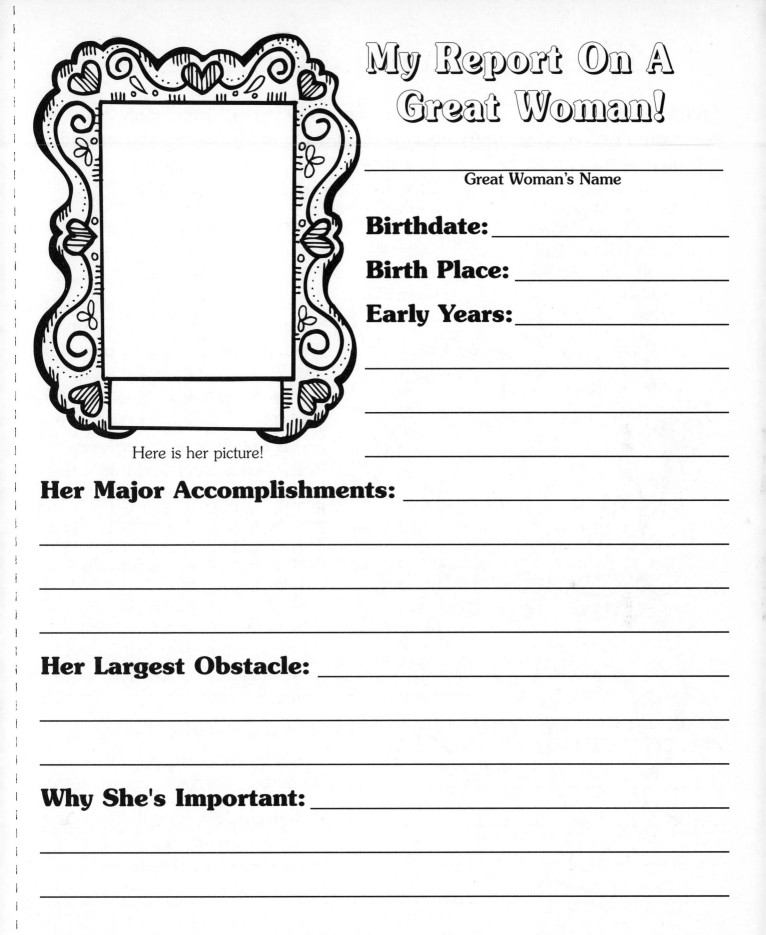

Here is her picture!

_____
Great Woman's Name

Birthdate: _____

Birth Place: _____

Early Years: _____

_____

_____

_____

Her Major Accomplishments: _____

_____

_____

_____

Her Largest Obstacle: _____

_____

_____

Why She's Important: _____

_____

_____

_____

Famous Women Concentration!

Students will love to learn more about Famous Women in History with this "Concentration" activity. At the same time, students will be developing valuable memory skills.

Mount the card sets on poster board and laminate for greater wear.

Two students can play the game by shuffling the cards and laying them facedown on a table top. Each player takes turns revealing two cards at a time, trying to match the famous-woman card with her achievement card. If the cards match, the player keeps them and selects again until the cards do not match. Cards that do not match are returned to their exact spot and the player forfeits his or her turn to the other player.

The game continues until all cards are matched. The player with the most cards wins the game.

Additional cards can easily be made by assigning a famous woman to each student in class.

Ask each child to write the name of their woman on a pre-cut square of poster board and her accomplishments on another.

Play the same game as described above.

Susan B. Anthony

Elizabeth Cady Stanton

Clara Barton

Harriet Tubman

Eleanor Roosevelt

Amelia Earhart

Wilma Rudolph

Helen Keller

Sandra Day O'Connor

Sojourner Truth

Babe Didrikson

Sacagawea

TF0300 March Idea Book

This talented Olympic athlete was one of 19 children. She overcame childhood paralysis to win three gold medals during the 1960 Olympic games.

This woman was born both deaf and blind. She overcame her handicaps and taught herself to speak. She gave numerous lectures across the country that were dedicated to changing society's attitude toward the disabled.

This woman was named the first female Supreme Court Justice of the United States.

This woman was born into slavery but later spoke out for human rights. She traveled the country speaking at anti-slavery meetings and helped ex-slaves rebuild their lives as free people.

This woman was the first female Olympic champion. She won gold medals in the 80m, hurdles, and javelin, and a silver medal in the high jump during the 1932 Games.

Without this Native American woman, explorers Lewis and Clark might have never completed their journey of the northwest region of the U.S. She served them as both guide and interpreter during their 8,000 mile expedition.

This woman was a determined crusader for women's right to vote. She was once arrested for attempting to vote. Her face appears on the dollar coin.

This woman organized the first Women's Rights Convention. She encouraged other women to fight for the right to own property, obtain an education and to vote and hold office.

This courageous woman tended wounded soldiers during the Civil War. She later organized the American Red Cross, which provides relief during both wartime and peacetime emergencies.

Before the outbreak of the Civil War, this escaped slave made a total of nineteen trips to the South to lead other slaves to freedom. She was later known as the "Moses" of her people.

This president's wife devoted herself to a career of social reform. After her husband's death, she was appointed the U.S. representative to the United Nations and later became chairperson of the Human Rights Commission.

This woman's love of flying led her to many "firsts." She was both the first woman to earn a pilot's license and the first woman to fly solo across the Atlantic Ocean.

Eleanor Roosevelt

Helen Keller

Sacagawea

 TF0300 March Idea Book

Susan B. Anthony

Wilma
Rudolph

Amelia
Earhart

Music Appreciation!

MUSIC MANIA!

83

Music Month Activities!

Celebrate music in your classroom by encouraging your students to appreciate different types of music and the creative process by which music is created. Try some of these musical activities with your students.

SINGING TELEGRAMS

The first singing telegram was delivered in New York City on February 10, 1933. Ask your students to write and perform their own singing telegrams.

Select a familiar tune such as "Old MacDonald" or "Three Blind Mice." Instruct students to choose someone as the telegram's subject. Have them write their own lyrics to one of the tunes on the form in this chapter. Let the students perform the singing telegrams in front of the class.

PIANO EXAMINATION

If you have access to a class piano, let your students have a close look at how it works.

Remove the front panel of an upright piano to reveal the complex system of strings and hammers. As a group, count the strings. Ask them to watch the hammers as you press a key. Instruct them to notice what happens when the key is released. Show them that it is the "damper" that presses against the string to silence it.

Let each child take a turn pressing one key at a time. Help the students point out which string is hit.

Bring other music instruments to class that can be examined and tried by each child in class.

CLASS-MADE MUSIC MAKERS

Children love making their own music. They also love using instruments they make themselves. Try some of these ideas:

• Decorate an empty coffee can with a plastic lid. Thump the plastic lid to create a drum sound.

• Place a handful of dry beans in two small, empty coffee cans with plastic lids to make a set of maracas.

• Cover two small blocks of wood with sandpaper. Rub them together lightly to make a swish-swish sound.

• A piece of waxed paper wrapped around a fine-toothed comb makes a great instrument. Hold the comb, teeth up, between your lips and hum a tune. The teeth and paper vibrate, creating a kazoolike sound.

• Hold a pair of spoons, back to back, between your fingers. Tap the spoons on your knee to create a clickety-click sound. (The secret is to hold them lightly.)

Music Month Activities!

MUSIC VOCABULARY

Write the following music vocabulary words on colorful paper and give each student one word to research. Arrange the words, along with their definitions, on the class board and ask students to select six words to include in a creative writing assignment.

CONCERT	CONDUCTOR
CHORUS	ORCHESTRA
HARMONY	SOPRANO
ALTO	TENOR
QUARTET	BALLAD
JAZZ	OPERA
SYMPHONY	VIOLIN
CELLO	HARP
FLUTE	PICCOLO
OBOE	CLARINET
BASSOON	PERCUSSION
TROMBONE	TRUMPET
TUBA	CYMBALS

SOUND AND MUSIC

Music instruments make their sound by vibrating the air. However, each instrument does it in a different way. String instruments have strings that vibrate. Wood instruments have reeds that vibrate. Percussion instruments vibrate when someone strikes them. The vibrations from brass instruments come from the player's lips.

The type of sound created depends on how slow or fast the air vibrates. A low sound is made by slow vibrations. A high sound is made by fast vibrations.

Demonstrate several sounds to your class and ask them to determine if they are low sounds or high sounds.

BODY MOVEMENT NOTES

Teach your youngsters the musical scale including these body movements.

DO - Touch the floor with your hands.
RE - Put your hands on your knees.
MI - Put your hands on your hips.
FA - Put your hands on your waist.
SO - Put your hands on your shoulders.
LA - Put your hands on your head.
TI - Stretch your hands straight out.
DO - Stretch your hands straight up.

Repeat the scale several times. When the children have perfected the scale and the movements, encourage them to perform it faster and faster.

WATER XYLOPHONE

Make this simple music instrument and let your students experiment with the various tones.

Begin by using eight identical one-quart jars or drinking glasses. Number each of the jars. Fill jar number one with a little water, number two with slightly more, number three with still more and so on. Arrange the jars in order and strike each one with a wooden mallet or wooden spoon. Use a pitch pipe or piano to set the pitch of each jar. (Use more or less water as needed.)

Let children tap out their own tunes or try one of these old favorites using the numbers below.

"Row, Row, Row Your Boat"
1 1   1 2 3   3 2 4   5   8 8 8
5 5 5   3 3 3 1 1   5 4 3 2   1

"Mary Had A Little Lamb"
6 2 1 2 6 6   6   2 2 2   6 6   6
6 2 1 2 6 6   6 6 2 2 6 2 1

SINGING TELEGRAM

To:_____

From: _____

Message: _____

_____

_____

_____

_____

_____

_____

Sing to the tune of:

_____

_____

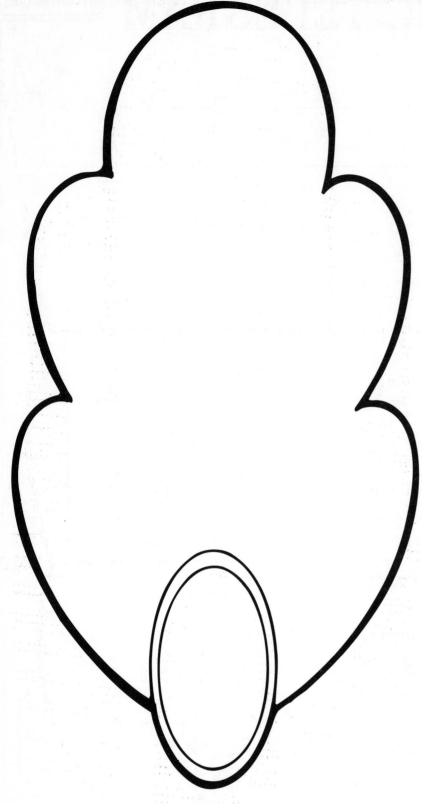

Marching Band Hat

Color and cut the Marching Band Hat and feather from construction paper. Paste the feather in place. Fold the hat's bill outward and attach it to a paper headband.

Have students make their own music makers. They can then wear their Marching Band Hats and parade around the classroom or school grounds.

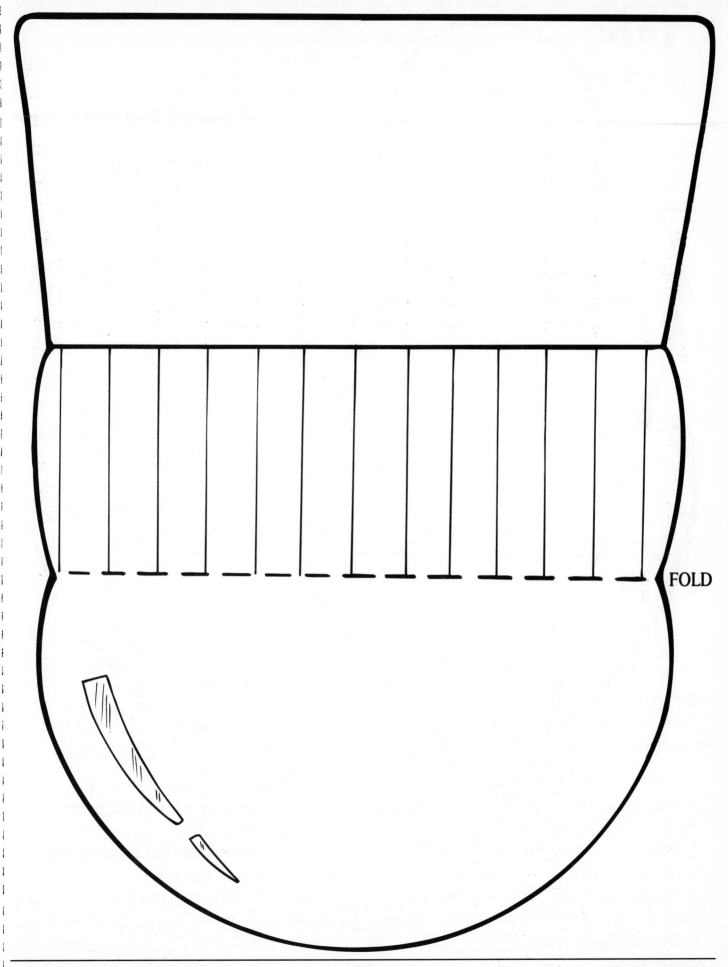

FOLD

Tuba Teddy

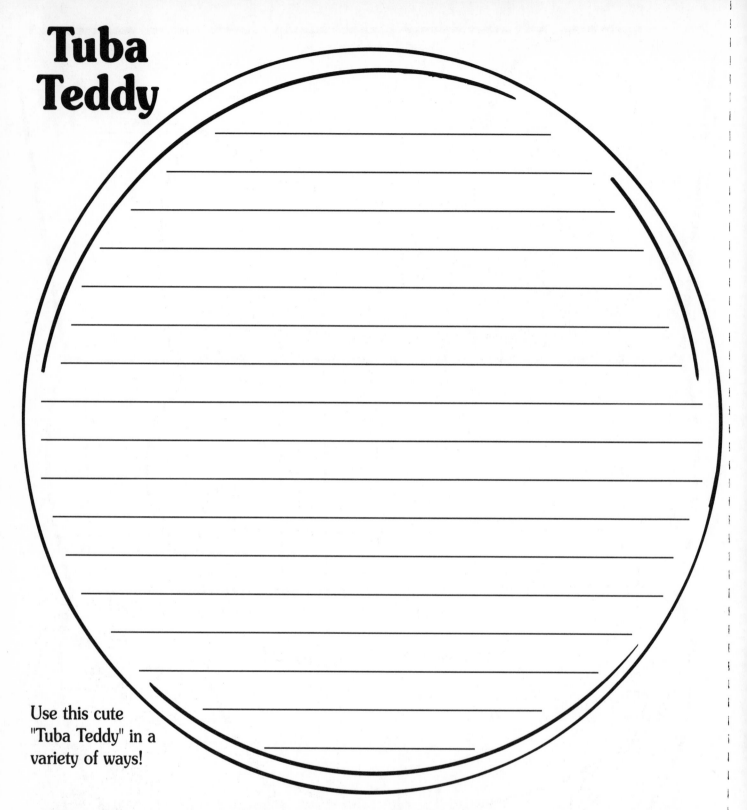

Use this cute "Tuba Teddy" in a variety of ways!

1. Enlarge the patterns and display them on the class board with one of the following titles: "Students Who Are Blowing Their Own Horns!" or "Take Note of This!"
2. Give each student "Tuba Teddy" and have them each write music vocabulary words or spelling words on the horn.
3. Display one "Tuba Teddy" for each student on the class bulletin board. Award students paper musical notes when work is completed or behavior improves. Students can pin the notes around their own tubas!

Patrick

TF0300 March Idea Book

Music Word Find!

ACTIVITY 4

FIND THESE MUSIC WORDS IN THE
PUZZLE BELOW:

SONG
NOTE
TUNE
INSTRUMENT
MUSIC
PIANO
BAND
MUSICIAN
HORN
VIOLIN
DRUM
ORCHESTRA

```
I N S T R U M E N T E A T O N M
I V O Y U E O I U A H J N C U U
E J B C Y U I O H J C Y U I B S
E J A N G H U R B J T H Q W E I
T Y N I O D P C D R U M J Y G C
H N D L K D J H K N P J K H U I
S B E D N M B E J A Z J D F L A
E U Y R I O F S J H D K F J D H
F J B C M N H T K A D H F E U H
M N N O T E W R H O R N D V U E
Y R H I J D V A N V I O L I N D
H B J F H E U F D H B C J H S P
I U E H A L A K J H D F L A I I
O Q O B I W U E O I U H D K J A
S I E A H R J X T U N E C V I N
O E I G A C I V N E W O I R N O
N K J D F A O W E U R Q P O I D
G M U S I C I A N W E R U I K N
```

Music Instrument Match!

Help your students identify different
music instruments with the cards on
the following pages.

Children can match the pictures to the
names of the instruments. They can
also separate the instruments into the
categories of percussion, brass, wood-
winds, and strings.

Encourage the children to find other
pictures of instruments to make their
own cards.

guitar

violin

French horn

trumpet

drum

cymbals

flute

clarinet

Japan!

Japan!

The people of Japan live in a culture of ancient traditions and modern technologies. The Japanese people ride on the fastest trains in the world and produce some of the world's most advanced computers, automobiles, televisions and cameras. At the same time, they have great respect for the traditions handed down to them by their elders. They are known to appreciate beauty and nature, have great respect for older people and strive daily to be polite and peaceful.

Bring the atmosphere of the Japanese culture to your students by providing them with a variety of resource books on Japan. You may want to have them sample some Japanese foods or invite them to participate in a Japanese tea ceremony.

JAPANESE POETRY - HAIKU

For hundreds of years, Japanese poets have written a special form of poetry called a haiku. A haiku is a short verse about nature. There is a special pattern to the number of syllables used in a haiku. The first line always contains five syllables, the second line has seven and the third line has five. Ask your students to count the number of syllables in this haiku poem.

> The soft warm sunshine
> gently opens pink petals
> with the hope of peace.

Instruct your students to write their own haiku poems using one of these topics:

raindrops	a pond of water	trees	birds
wind	butterflies	flowers	lightning
the ocean	springtime	honeybees	grass
a garden	fireflies	rabbits	mountains

Have your students make haiku booklets for their poems. Ask them to illustrate their poems on the folded pages.

You will need:
Two pieces of cardboard (3" x 4")   20" of adding machine tape
Enough giftwrap or wallpaper to   A piece of ribbon (20" long)
cover both sides of the cardboard.

Cover the two cardboard pieces with giftwrap paper and glue the ribbon to the back of the piece that will become the back cover of the booklet.

Fold the adding machine tape into six equal parts as shown. Glue the ends to the two pieces of covered cardboard.

When dry, fold the booklet together and tie with a ribbon. Write your own haiku poem inside.

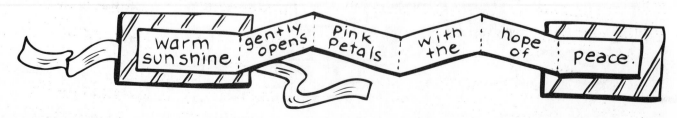

Japanese Festivals!

HINA-MATSURI DOLL FESTIVAL

On March 3rd, Japanese girls dress up in their finest kimonos and display beautiful doll collections. These dolls are passed down from grandmothers and mothers to the girls in the family. Visitors are invited to see the collection and served tea and sweet cakes.

Invite both the girls and boys in your class to bring in their favorite dolls or action heros to display in class on March 3rd.

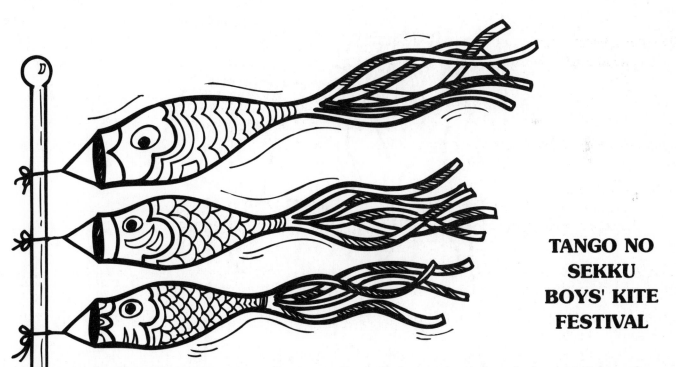

TANGO NO SEKKU BOYS' KITE FESTIVAL

On May 5th, Japanese boys attach fish kites (windsocks) to tall bamboo poles and fly the colorful kites in the family garden. There is usually one kite flown for each boy in the family.

On this day, let all of the students in your class fly kites on the school playground.

Japan

Japan

Torii Gate

Torii gates are found throughout Japan. They mark the entry to Japanese shrines.

It is considered good luck to walk under a Torii gate. They are usually painted red, also a symbol of good luck.

Cut a large Torii gate from red craft paper and display it around your classroom door during the month of March.

Fish Kite

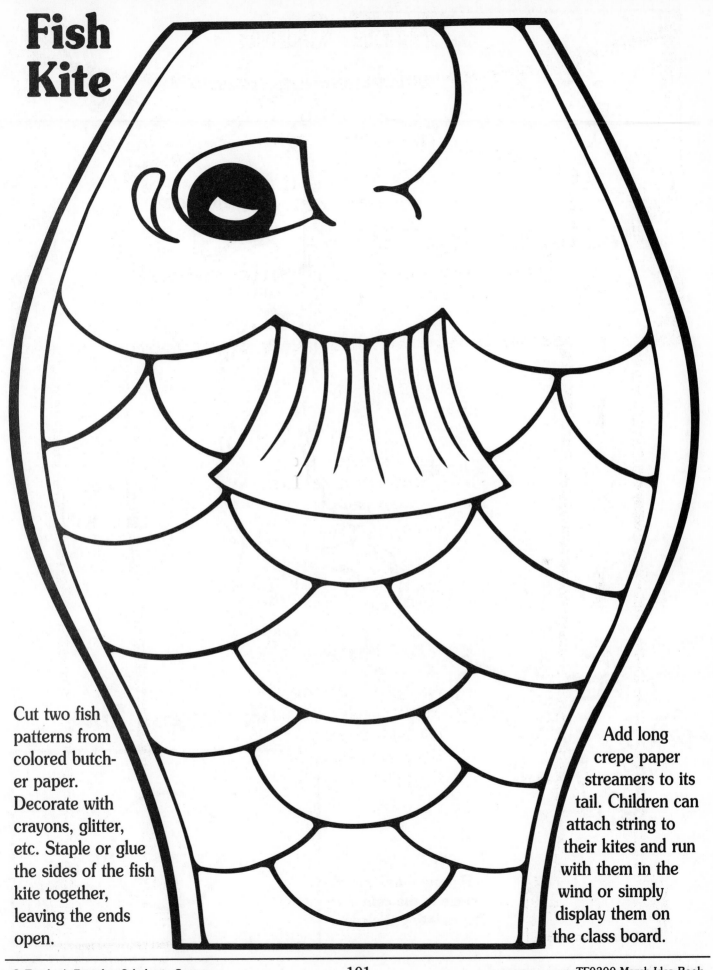

Cut two fish patterns from colored butcher paper. Decorate with crayons, glitter, etc. Staple or glue the sides of the fish kite together, leaving the ends open.

Add long crepe paper streamers to its tail. Children can attach string to their kites and run with them in the wind or simply display them on the class board.

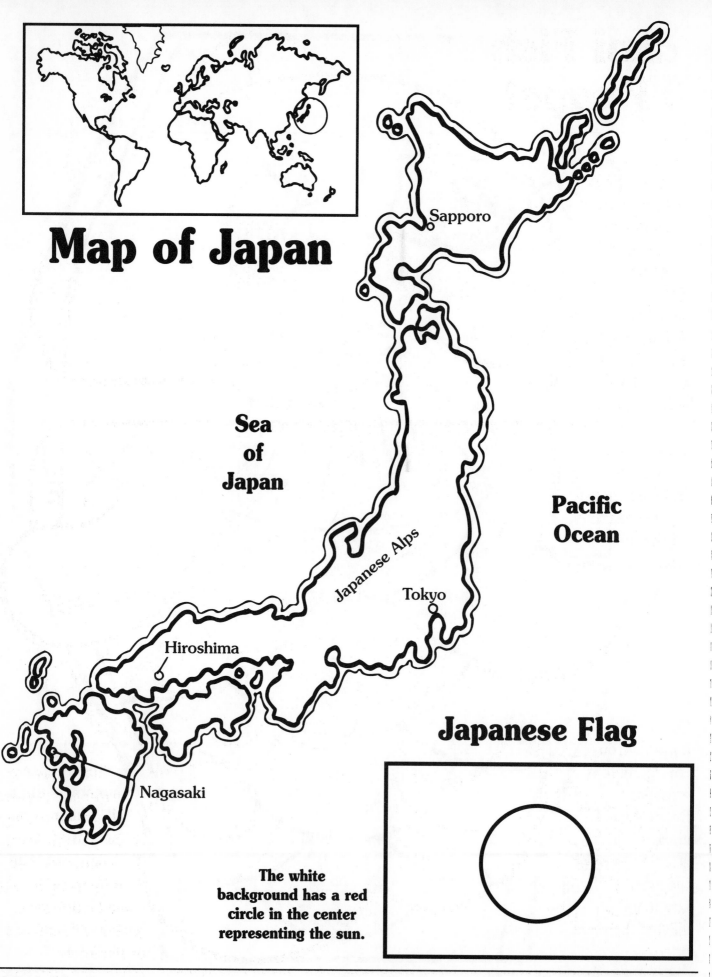

Map of Japan

Sapporo

Sea
of
Japan

Pacific
Ocean

Japanese Alps

Tokyo

Hiroshima

Nagasaki

Japanese Flag

The white background has a red circle in the center representing the sun.

TF0300 March Idea Book

Koi Fish Puppet

To the Japanese people, the koi fish, or carp, is a symbol of courage and strength. On May 5th, families fly fish kites from flag-poles. Each kite represents one boy in the family. It is hoped that each child will devel-op the qualities of the much-admired koi.

Make this fish paperbag puppet by simply cutting the pattern from construction paper and pasting it to a small lunch sack. Color with crayons or markers.

TF0300 March Idea Book

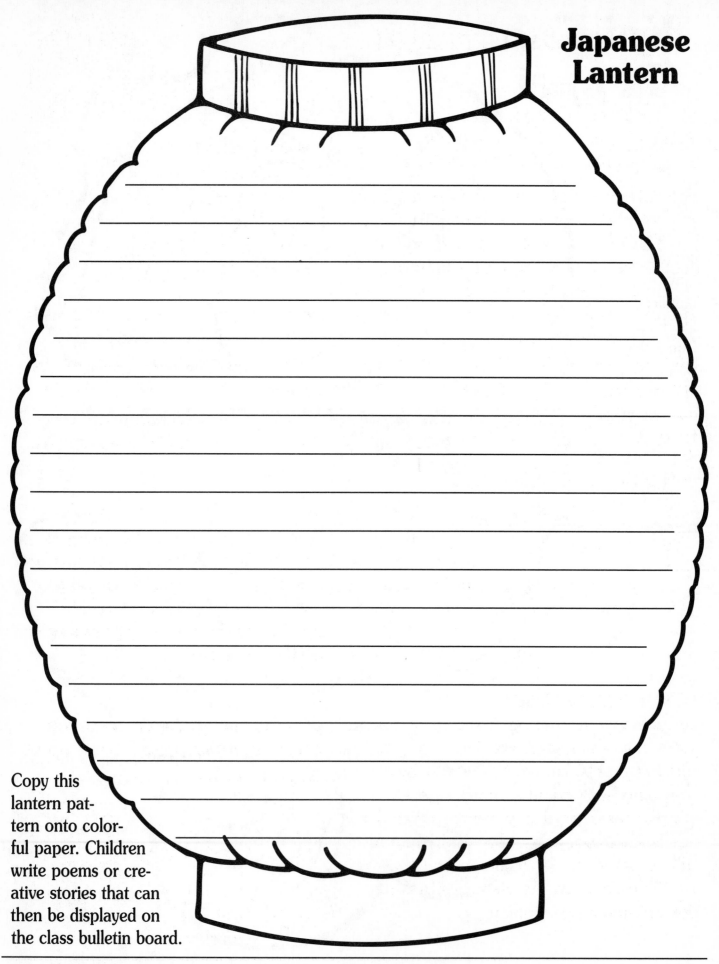

Japanese Lantern

Copy this lantern pattern onto colorful paper. Children write poems or creative stories that can then be displayed on the class bulletin board.

Japanese Crafts!

ABACUS

For hundreds of years, Asians have used a counting tool called an abacus to figure mathematical calculations.

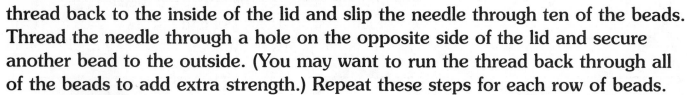

You can make an abacus by using a box lid and thirty-six beads or buttons. Punch three small holes in each end of your box lid. With a needle, pull heavy thread through one hole and secure one bead to the outside of the box. Pull the thread back to the inside of the lid and slip the needle through ten of the beads. Thread the needle through a hole on the opposite side of the lid and secure another bead to the outside. (You may want to run the thread back through all of the beads to add extra strength.) Repeat these steps for each row of beads.

Count the beads, one at a time, or do simple arithmetic problems. Young children will easily see that seven beads taken from ten leaves three.

JAPANESE FAN

Make a Japanese fan using a 9" x 12" piece of construction paper. Draw flowers or designs on both sides of the paper. Use chalk, crayons or colored markers. Fold the paper every 1/2" making fan pleats. Staple the pleats together at one end to form your Japanese fan.

LOTUS BLOSSOMS

Lotus blossoms can be found in ponds and lakes throughout Japan every summer. Have your students cut three petal patterns from white paper. Ask them to curl the petals toward the center by wrapping each petal around a pencil. Instruct them to glue the three layers of petals together, as shown, and paste a yellow paper circle to the center. Pin the lotus blossoms to the class board for a flowery Japanese display.

Pearl and Oyster

Pearls are known in Japan as "the gift of kings." If possible, bring to class a string of pearls and a few oysters from a local fish market. (Make sure you open an oyster so they can see the insides.) Explain that in nature a small grain of sand often gets inside the oyster's shell. This grain of sand becomes an irritant and over time it becomes an iridescent pearl.

Ask students to find out about the pearl divers of Japan. Have them find out why they wear white and for how long they can hold their breath. Ask them also to find out how cultured pearls are made.

Cut two

Pearl

Cut these two oyster patterns from colored paper and staple them together at the base. Cut the pearl from white paper and insert it into the oyster.

Make a matching activity by having students write questions about sea life on the oysters and answers on the pearls. They may then match the pearls to the appropriate oysters.

Farm Animals!

Farm Animals in the Classroom!

Children will love learning about various barnyard animals and farm life with the following activities and patterns.

ANIMALS IN THE CLASSROOM
Contact your local Farm Bureau, 4-H Club or Future Farmers of America. You should be able to locate a volunteer who will bring a few farm animals to your classroom for the children to pet and observe. Baby chicks, rabbits or perhaps a piglet will delight your youngsters.

You may also want to have your class visit a local farm or dairy. Ask parent volunteers to help organize the children for the trip. Take photos of the visit and arrange them, along with student drawings and writings, to make a display of farm activities.

PIGGY POEMS
Write this favorite childhood poem on the class board.

This little piggy went to the market.
This little piggy stayed home.
This little piggy had roast beef.
This little piggy had none.
This little piggy went wee-wee-wee
All the way home!

Ask children to revise the poem. They may want to use a different farm animal besides a pig. An example might be:

This little duck ate ice cream.
This little duck ate pie.
This little duck ate pizza.
This little duck asked why.
This little duck went quack-quack-quack
All the way to the pond!

FARM TASK CARDS
Here are a few ideas for creative writing assignments or simple task activities:

Make a list of adult farm animals and their youngsters.

"Which came first, the chicken or the egg?" Write about your ideas.

Write a letter to a local farmer.

List the various jobs that are required on a farm.

Write a story about: "How the duck got his quack!" "How the cow got her moo!" "How the chicken got her cluck!"

FARMYARD MATCH
Young children will love playing this "rainy day" game. Select one student to be the "farmer" and ask him/her to think of three different farm animals. Instruct him/her to whisper the name of one of the animals to each child in class. With their eyes closed, tell students to make the appropriate animal sounds. Ask them to link arms when they find other members of their group.

Farm Animals in the Classroom!

MAKING BUTTER

Before beginning this tasty experiment, discuss with your children the differences between solids and liquids. You should also explain that milk comes from cows, and that cream and ultimately butter comes from milk.

With the children seated in a circle, pour a 1/2 pint of heavy whipping cream (not super pasteurized) and a dash of salt into a clear plastic container with a tight fitting lid. Pass the container around the circle and have each child shake it a few times. When everyone has had a turn, open the container and have the students observe any changes to the liquid. (Are there bubbles in the liquid? Does it appear thicker? What color is it?)

Keep passing the container around the circle with each child taking a turn at shaking. Keep opening the container periodically, noting any changes. Soon the cream will turn to whipped cream and then finally to butter. It will also go from a white liquid to a yellowish solid. Give each student a small amount served on a cracker or small piece of bread.

ANIMAL SAYINGS

Ask your students to write their own creative meanings for these common sayings.

"Got Your Goat"	"Whole Hog"
"Hold Your Horses"	"Horse Sense"
"Don't Chicken Out"	"Hog Heaven"
"Chicken-Hearted"	"Dog-Tired"
"Don't Horse Around"	"Talk Turkey"
"Mule-Headed"	"Bull-Headed"
"Hog Wash"	
"From the Horse's Mouth"	

FARM ANIMAL PRODUCTS

Enlarge the farm animal illustrations in this chapter and display them on the class board. After a class discussion regarding farm animals and the products they provide, write those products on colored paper and pin them above the animals. Students can match each animal to the products they provide with a length of yarn. Here are some products to include:

cow	milk, cheese, butter
pig	ham, bacon
chicken	eggs, feathers, meat
goat	milk, cheese
sheep	wool, meat
duck	eggs, feathers

PIG PEN

Turn a corner of your classroom into an intriguing "Pig Pen!" Section the area off with a cardboard fence or a small picket garden fence (found in your local hardware store). Add a few throw pillows and a cardboard box trough. Fill the trough with a selection of "piggy" literature books. Kids will love "pigging out" during silent reading time!

Animal Families!

Read the names of each male, female and young farm animal. Ask students to identify the family name. Students may want to research additional animals.

Family	Male	Female	Young
Cat	Tom	Queen	Kitten
Cattle	Bull	Cow	Calf
Deer	Buck	Doe	Fawn
Dog	Sire	Bitch	Puppy
Duck	Drake	Duck	Duckling
Goose	Gander	Goose	Gosling
Horse	Stallion	Mare	Foal
Mule	Jack	Jenny	Foal
Rabbit	Buck	Doe	Bunny
Sheep	Ram	Ewe	Lamb
Swine	Boar	Sow	Piglet

You may want to write the various names in each group on slips of paper and pass the names out to your students. Instruct children to try to find those students with coordinating names to complete the animal group. Example: Duck, Duck, Drake and Duckling.

Barnyard Bingo!

Write the following list of farm animals names on the class board. Ask students to write any 24 animal names on his or her bingo card. Use the same directions as you might for regular bingo with one additional rule: Tell the children that they must make the sound of the given animal when its name is called if they have it on their bingo card!

COW	HEN	DOG	LAMB	PUPPY	FROG
SHEEP	CHICK	CAT	CALF	MULE	MOUSE
PIG	HOG	BARN OWL	PIGLET	KITTY	TURKEY
DONKEY	BULL	GOAT	RABBIT	DUCKLING	KID
DUCK	HORSE	GOOSE	COLT	BUNNY	ROOSTER

BARNYARD
BINGO

FREE

Farm Animals Patterns

Give each student a copy of the barn on the following page.

Have students cut out the window and doors, color with crayons and paste it on a folded piece of construction paper to make a booklet.

Farm animal patterns can then be cut out and pasted inside the barn pattern. Stories about farm animals can be written inside the booklet.

TF0300 March Idea Book

Name

Piggy
Booklet

Matching Hen and Nest

Cut several copies of each pattern from construction paper. Write a number on the hen's wing and paste the same number of eggs in the nest. Children can match the hen to the appropriate nest with the correct number of eggs.

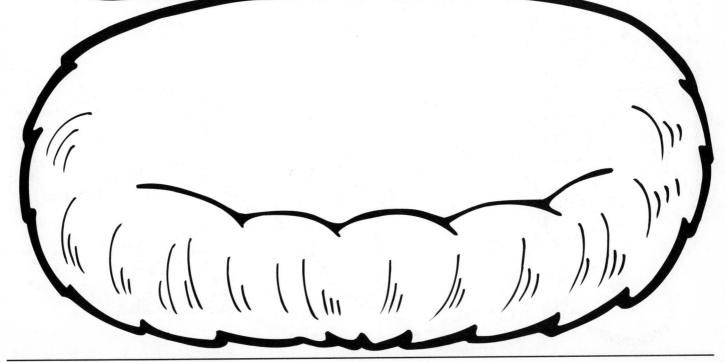

Pig
Puppet

Have students use these cute barnyard animal puppets to act out simple plays they write themselves!

TF0300 March Idea Book

Cow
Puppet

Young children will have fun imitating the sounds of farm animals with these paperbag puppets.

Duck Puppet

Let each child choose a barnyard animal puppet to make. Instruct students to write stories or poems about their animal.

Certificate of Achievement

Name

Teacher

Date

Cow Character

Mount these cow patterns around creative writing pages or enlarge it to display around the class bulletin board.

Rainbow of Colors!

Rainbow of Colors Activities!

Celebrate the spring season with one or more of these colorful activities!

COLOR DAY

Liven up a dreary winter day by devoting it to a color. Here are a few ideas:

- Ask children to come to school dressed in the chosen color.
- Have them do art projects with the color.
- Make a list of objects associated with the color.
- Discuss emotions and feelings associated with the color.
- Write a poem about the color.
- Bring in foods the chosen color for the students to sample.

After several "Color Days" ask students to vote for their favorite color and graph the results.

INVITE A PRINTER

Ask a local printer to come to your class and explain the process of printing everything from books to posters, and newspapers to magazines. They will probably be able to bring a "color key" or color separation to illustrate how printers print all the colors of the rainbow by using only four colors.

COLOR WORDS

Write color words on strips of paper and distribute one to each child in class. Tell the students to keep their color word a secret while they orally list objects that are their specific color. Classmates can guess the color associated with the objects named. For young children use only the basic colors. Older students can use more descriptive colors such as:

avocado	orchid	mustard
cocoa	aqua	gold
fuchsia	ebony	tan
emerald	pumpkin	eggshell
peach	ivory	mint
burgundy	canary	midnight
lime	navy	grape
lavender	coffee	sand

MAKE A RAINBOW

Begin by explaining to your class that light is made up of all the colors of the rainbow. When light passes through water, the water separates the colors and becomes visible as in a rainbow. Illustrate this phenomenon with this simple experiment:

On a sunny day, place a clear glass of water on a table, position the glass so that it is half on the table and half off. Make sure that sunlight coming from a window shines directly through the glass and onto the floor. Place a large white sheet of paper on the floor in line with the sunlight and watch a rainbow appear.

Children can also make rainbows by blowing bubbles outside on a sunny day.

Rainbow of Colors Activities!

RAINBOW GAME
Arrange chairs in a circle, making sure you have one less chair than the number of children playing the game. Select one student to stand in the center of the circle. Ask the other students to each sit in a chair. Give every student a slip of colored paper. (Each color should be different, with the name of the color written boldly on the slip.) The student standing in the center calls out the name of two colors. The children with those colors must try to change places before the person in the middle can get their chair. The student left without a chair takes the position in the center and the game continues.

Every now and then, instruct the person in the middle to call out, "Rainbow!" When this happens, everyone must try to get a new chair.

HISTORY IN COLOR
Bring "color" to the sometimes dull facts of history. Have children choose one of the following "colorful" historical facts, people, monuments or events to research. Mount the papers on the appropriate colored paper and display them on the class board.

The California Gold Rush
The Blue and the Grey
The White House
The Green Berets
The Redcoats
Yellowstone National Park
The Red, White and Blue

COLORFUL CREATIVE WRITING
Write on slips of paper names of objects that denote color. Pass out the slips of paper and ask students to write poems or "colorful" paragraphs about their objects. Here are a few ideas:

A Hot Stove	Cold Water
Dark Night	Summer Grass
Lemonade	Jack 'O Lantern
Chocolate Cake	Bunch of Bananas
Strawberries	Pine Tree
Vanilla Ice Cream	Sunny Day

COLORFUL PARAGRAPHS
Help your older students learn the various parts of a paragraph with this colorful idea.

Make copies of a variety of magazine or newspaper articles and provide colored highlight pens for each student.

Ask students to highlight the main idea of the article with one color. Have them highlight the main points another color and the conclusive statement a third color. Children can display the colorful articles on the class board.

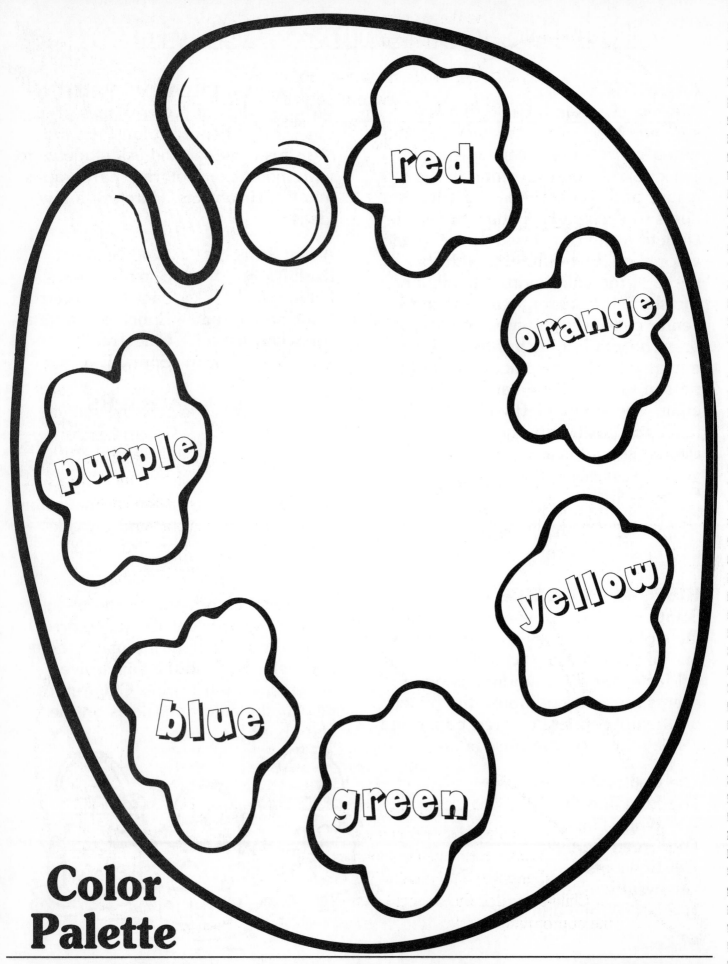

Color
Palette

124

Use these color palette patterns in a variety of ways in the classroom.

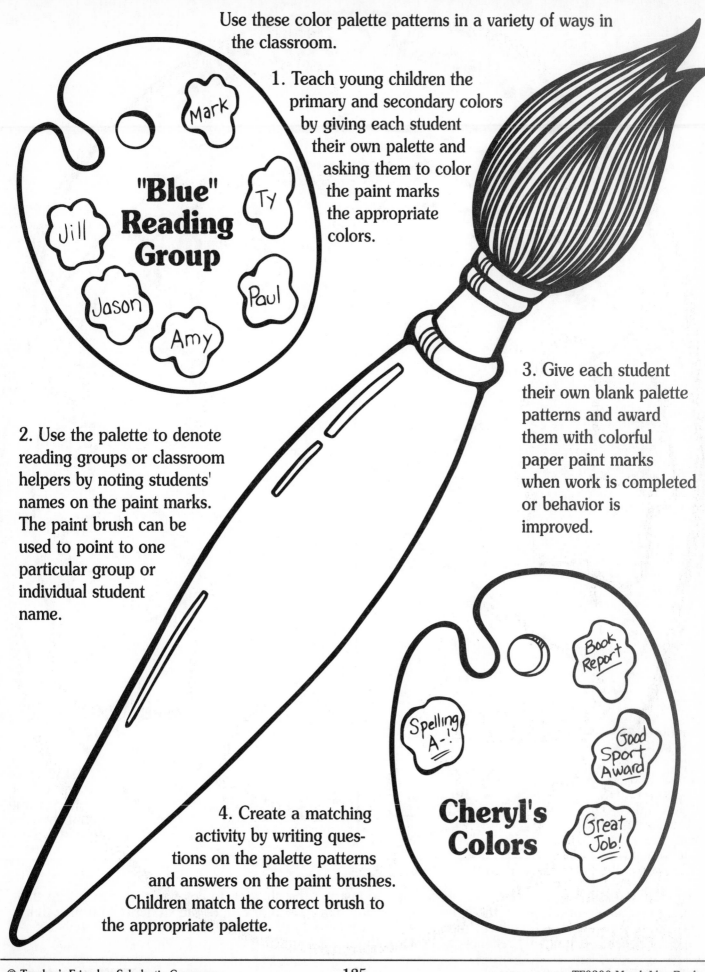

1. Teach young children the primary and secondary colors by giving each student their own palette and asking them to color the paint marks the appropriate colors.

"Blue" Reading Group

Mark
Ty
Jill
Jason
Amy
Paul

3. Give each student their own blank palette patterns and award them with colorful paper paint marks when work is completed or behavior is improved.

2. Use the palette to denote reading groups or classroom helpers by noting students' names on the paint marks. The paint brush can be used to point to one particular group or individual student name.

4. Create a matching activity by writing questions on the palette patterns and answers on the paint brushes. Children match the correct brush to the appropriate palette.

Cheryl's Colors

Spelling A-!
Book Report
Good Sport Award
Great Job!

My Personal Color Wheel

Name

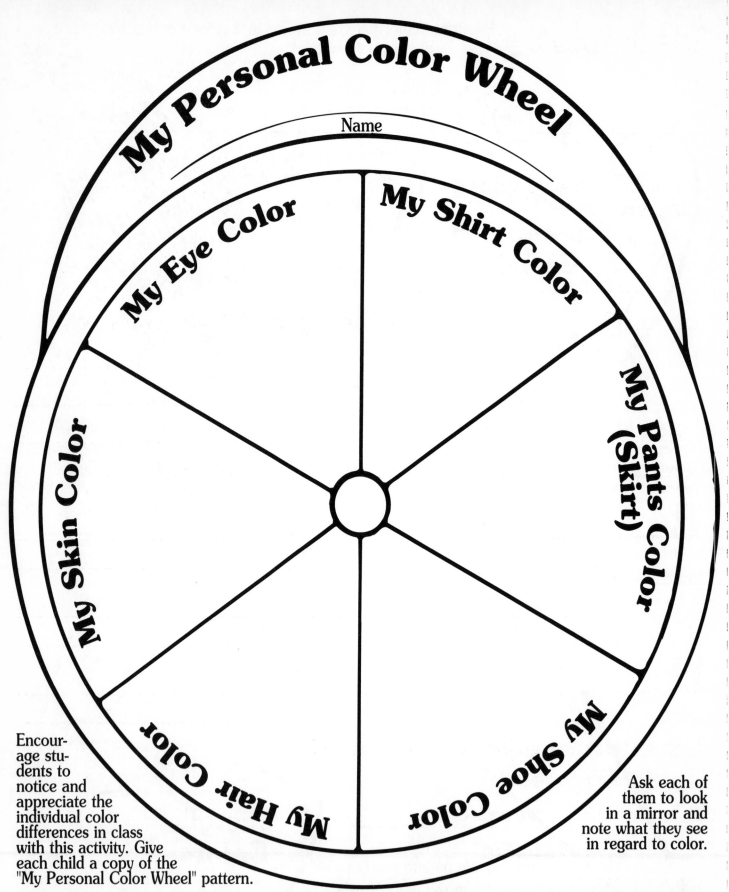

My Eye Color

My Shirt Color

My Pants Color (Skirt)

My Skin Color

My Hair Color

My Shoe Color

Encourage students to notice and appreciate the individual color differences in class with this activity. Give each child a copy of the "My Personal Color Wheel" pattern.

Ask each of them to look in a mirror and note what they see in regard to color.

Provide an extra large assortment of crayons and instruct the children to color in the wheels with their own personal colors. Display the wheels on the class board and ask all of the students to notice that no two wheels are exactly alike. Emphasize the large variety of colors. Tell them that each wheel is special because it uniquely reflects each one of them.

My Report on the Color

red

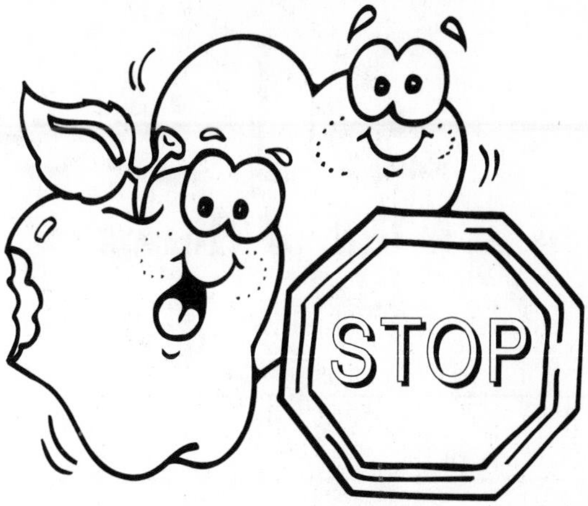

Here is a list of things that are red!

_____

_____

_____

_____

_____

Other names for the color red!

_____

_____

_____

Here's my poem using the letters in the word red!

R _____

_____

E _____

_____

D _____

_____

Colors can be either warm or cool.

Red is ☐ **cool**

☐ **warm**

Finish this sentence.

Red is like _____

_____.

My Report on the Color

_____
Student's Name

blue

Here is a list of things that are <u>blue</u>!

_____

_____

_____

_____

Other names for the color <u>blue</u>!

_____

_____

_____

Here's my poem using the letters in the word <u>blue</u>!

B _____

L _____

U _____

E _____

Colors can be either warm or cool.

    blue is ☐ **cool**

          ☐ **warm**

Finish this sentence.

Blue is like _____

_____.

My Report on the Color
yellow

Student's Name

Here is a list of things that are <u>yellow</u>!

_____

_____

_____

_____

_____

Other names for the color <u>yellow</u>!

_____

_____

Here's my poem using the letters in the word <u>yellow</u>!

Y _____

E _____

L _____

L _____

O _____

W _____

Colors can be either warm or cool.
Yellow is ☐ cool
☐ warm

Finish this sentence.

Yellow is like _____

_____.

My Report on the Color

green

Student's Name

Here is a list of things that are green!

_____
_____
_____
_____

Other names for the color green!

_____
_____

Here's my poem using the letters in the word green!

G _____

R _____

E _____

E _____

N _____

Colors can be either warm or cool.

Green is ☐ cool

☐ warm

Finish this sentence.

Green is like_____

_____.

My Report on the Color

orange

_____
Student's Name

Here is a list of things that are <u>orange</u>!

_____

_____

_____

_____

Other names for the color <u>orange</u>!

_____

_____

Here's my poem using the letters in the word <u>orange</u>!

O _____

R _____

A _____

N _____

G _____

E _____

Colors can be either warm or cool.
   Orange is ☐ **cool**
          ☐ **warm**

Finish this sentence.

Orange is like _____

_____.

131   TF0300 March Idea Book

My Report on the Color

purple

Student's Name

Here is a list of things that are <u>purple</u>!

_____
_____
_____
_____

Other names for the color <u>purple</u>!

_____
_____

Here's my poem using the letters in the word <u>purple</u>!

P _____

U _____

R _____

P _____

L _____

E _____

Colors can be either warm or cool.
   Purple is ☐ **cool**
              ☐ **warm**

Finish this sentence.

Purple is like _____

_____.

Bulletin Boards and More!

Luck of the Irish

Jenny

Joey

Judy

Kacie

Andy

Beth

Linda

Kevin

Jack

Mike

Bulletin Boards and More!

REAL POT 'O GOLD

Help children understand the real treasures in life with this simple bulletin board. Display a pot of gold, complete with shamrocks and a large, colorful rainbow. Ask students to write values and ideals that are "more precious than gold" on either the rainbow or the shamrocks.

RAINY DAY MOBILE

Disregard superstition and hang an open umbrella from the class ceiling. Ask each child to write a story or poem on a raindrop pattern and hang them from the umbrella. It's best to use thread or fishing line.

This rainy day display is especially effective when placed over a library table arranged with popular children's books.

SWING HIGH! THIS SPRING

Draw a large swing set on the class bulletin board and ask the students to draw pictures of themselves on art paper. Attach a paper swing to the back of each picture and display them on the board. Yarn can be used in place of the swings' ropes.

Bulletin Boards and More!

FAMOUS FEMALES

Ask students to collect pictures and information about famous women. Display these on the class bulletin board along with a large scroll entitled "FAMOUS FEMALES!"

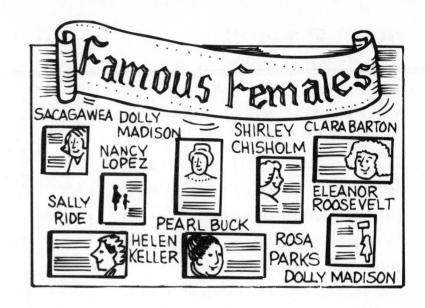

UP, UP AND AWAY!

Large paper circles are quickly transformed into balloons with this simple idea. Enlarge a cute illustration of a child and display it on the class bulletin board. Place the balloons on the board with long sections of yarn or kite string. Label the balloons with book titles, students' names, colors, etc.

RAINDROP WELCOME!

Welcome your students to school this spring with a cute paper umbrella and raindrops. Display each raindrop with the name of a student or ask each child to write a rainy day poem that can then be pinned to the board.

Bulletin Boards and More!

PICKET FENCE

Your students will love creating their own farm mural in the classroom. Assign each student one section of the mural. One student might be responsible for drawing the barn, while others each draw the cows, pigs, horses, etc. When the mural is complete, cut several fence posts from white paper. Give one fence post to each child and ask them to write "farm" poems or stories on the posts before displaying them on the mural.

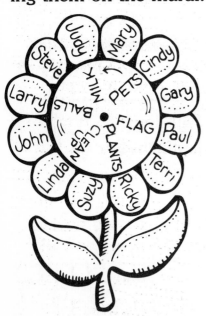

DAISY DUTIES

Cut one large construction paper circle and label it, as shown, with various classroom duties. Cut several smaller circles or petals, one for each member of the class. Arrange the "petals" around the larger circle. Rotate the center circle weekly in order give everyone in class a turn at the various jobs.

RACE THE RAINBOW...READ!

Display a colorful paper rainbow and fluffy white clouds on the class bulletin board. Student-made raindrops race from one end of the rainbow to the other as library books are read.

Bulletin Boards and More!

SPRING INTO ACTION
Display a cute leaping frog on a class bulletin board entitled "Spring into Action!" Tape small strips of fan-folded construction paper to the back of the frog to give him a "springy," 3-D effect. Display good work papers around the board.

FLYING HIGH!
Give each child in class their own kite pattern cut from colored construction paper. Have them write their names boldly on the kites and display them on the class board with long, white, crepe paper tails. As students complete assignments or improve behavior, award them a white paper bow noting their achievement. Pin the bows to the deserving student's kite tail. See who can earn the most bows within a given time.

WE'RE JAMMIN'!
Display a large jam jar on the class board. Cover the jar with clear plastic and staple the edges, leaving the top open. Cut dozens of paper strawberries and display them around the jar. When students do something worthy of recognition, reward them with a strawberry. The student writes his/her name on the berry and slips it into the jar. (The berries will be seen through the plastic sheeting.) At the end of the week or month, reach into the jar (with your eyes closed) and select one berry. That student receives a special prize. (Point out to the children that the more berries they have in the jar, the greater their chances of receiving the prize.)

Bulletin Board Murals!

Cover a large bulletin board with butcher paper and ask students to draw appropriate murals using colored chalk. Each day, more detail can be added. Students will love adding farm animals, leprechauns or fish kites to the completed projects.

Kite Pattern

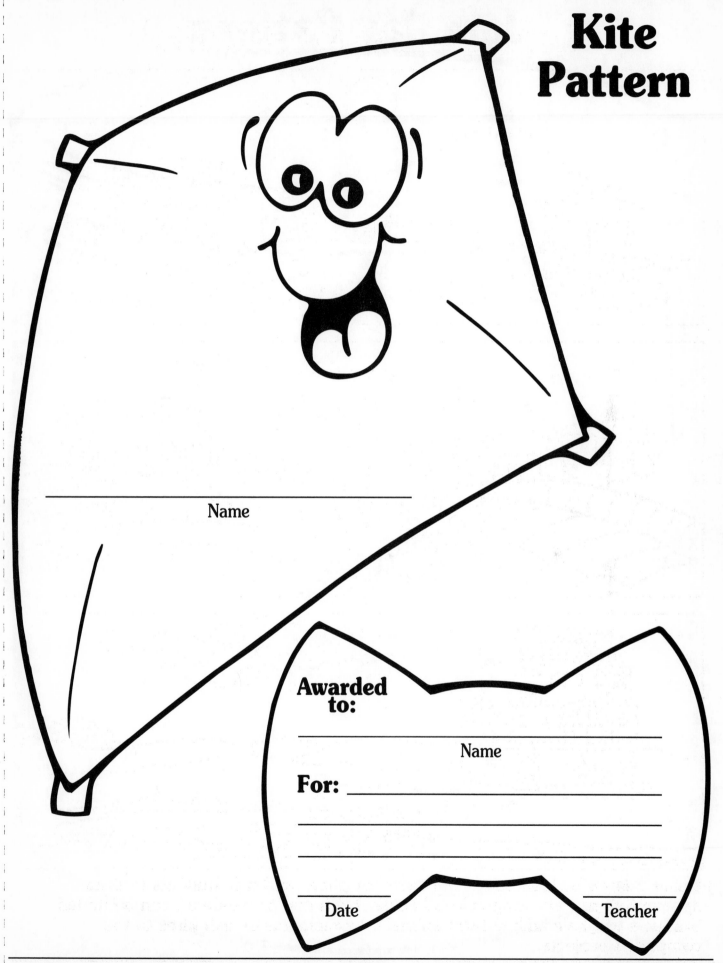

Name

Awarded to:
_____
Name

For: _____

_____

_____

_____
Date

Teacher

Jam Jar Pattern

Strawberry Pattern

"Berry" Good!

_____
Name

_____

_____

_____

_____
Teacher

_____
Date

Frog Patterns

Up, Up and Away!

BALLOONS

Tie kite string to paper balloons and attach the end of the strings to this kid's hand.

Give each child in class their own "kid" pattern. Students can earn colorful paper balloons as they complete assignments.

       TF0300 March Idea Book

Answer Key!

ACTIVITY 1
March Saying!

March comes in like a lion and goes out like a lamb.

ACTIVITY 2
MATCH THESE IRISH WORDS TO THEIR MEANING!

GAELIC — Irish Language

BLARNEY STONE — Kiss it and receive good luck.

IRISH JIG — Lively Irish Dance

SHENANIGAN — Mischief or Trickery

GNOME — Dwarf that guards a precious treasure.

SHILLELAGH — Walking Stick

ERIN — Ireland

ACTIVITY 3
Famous Woman Word Find!

```
C V G T Y H J N T D C V B L A C K W E L L
H I D R D F G T Y H J U I K L O P M N H Y
I X C U D V K E L L E R S X A W V D R T H
S D E T I S F B U C K F T H Y U K I L O P
H S W H D S V B T S I S W E T U B M A N U
O S W E R D F G T Y N H E P B U R N D W Q
L W S R I S W V B N G H Y F R T Y H N M R
M C B N K D R F V R O O S E V E L T S C I
B A R X S B A R T O N C C V T Y H U J D D
S D O D O X V F G B A N U E L O S S W G E
C T S F N H W I L D E R S P A E W R T H Y
X Z S D F G B E T H U N E A B L A C K P R
R U D O L P H C F G S E T R V B N M K A I
A E A R H A R T S C F T Y K C V B N M R L
Z C D B G H S A C A G A W E A D C V B K Y
S D A V G T Y H J U I K L O P M B G Y S R
B V M A N T H O N Y V T Y U I R E W F D S
M K S F G B H N M J K L I U O C O N N O R
```

ACTIVITY 4
Music Word Find!

```
I N S T R U M E N T E A T O N M
I V O Y U E O I U A H J N C U U
E J B C Y U I O H J C Y U I B S
E J A N G H U R B J T H Q W E I
T Y N I O D P C D R U M J Y G C
H N D L K D J H K N P J K H U I
S B E D N M B E J A Z J D F L A
E U Y R I O F S J H D K F J D H
F J B C M N H T K A D H F E U H
M N N O T E W R H O R N D V U E
Y R H I J D V A N V I O L I N D
H B J F H E U F D H B C J H S P
I U E H A L A K J H D F L A I I
O Q O B I W U E O I U H D K J A
S I E A H R J X T U N E C V I N
O E I G A C I V N E W O I R N O
N K J D F A O W E U R Q P O I D
G M U S I C I A N W E R U I K N
```